∞ Also Channeled from CEC ∞

Films ∞

Mi Familia Es Tu Familia (Ant Dip)

Average Joe and the Lava Java

Oxygen Friendly Environment

Clowns VS Monsters

Nocturnal Jurk (The Search For Destiny)

Sulten Skogtrol

The Vamp and Angel Show

90-100ft Parametre

One Millimetre

Sometimes You Forget Your Head

The Mentality of Movie

The Johnny Shepard Show

Mysteries of the Unexplained - Bat Boy

Mutant Screen Tests

Literature ∞

Sketchbook, Volume 3: March 1996 ∞ April 1996

Sketchbook, Volume 2: December 1995 ∞ January 1996

Sketchbook, Volume 1: January 1993 ∞ February 1994

Inspirado Projecto

U8U: The Legend of USSU

Sounds ∞

Most sounds can be heard on www.soundcloud.com/cec

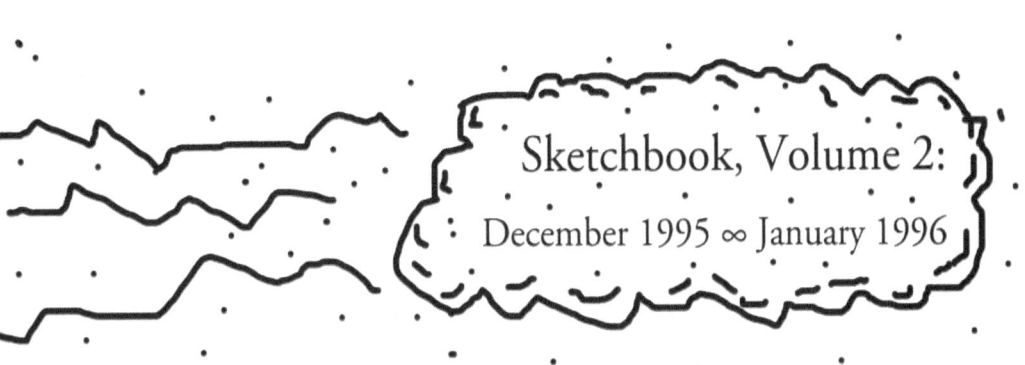

Sketchbook, Volume 2:

December 1995 ∞ January 1996

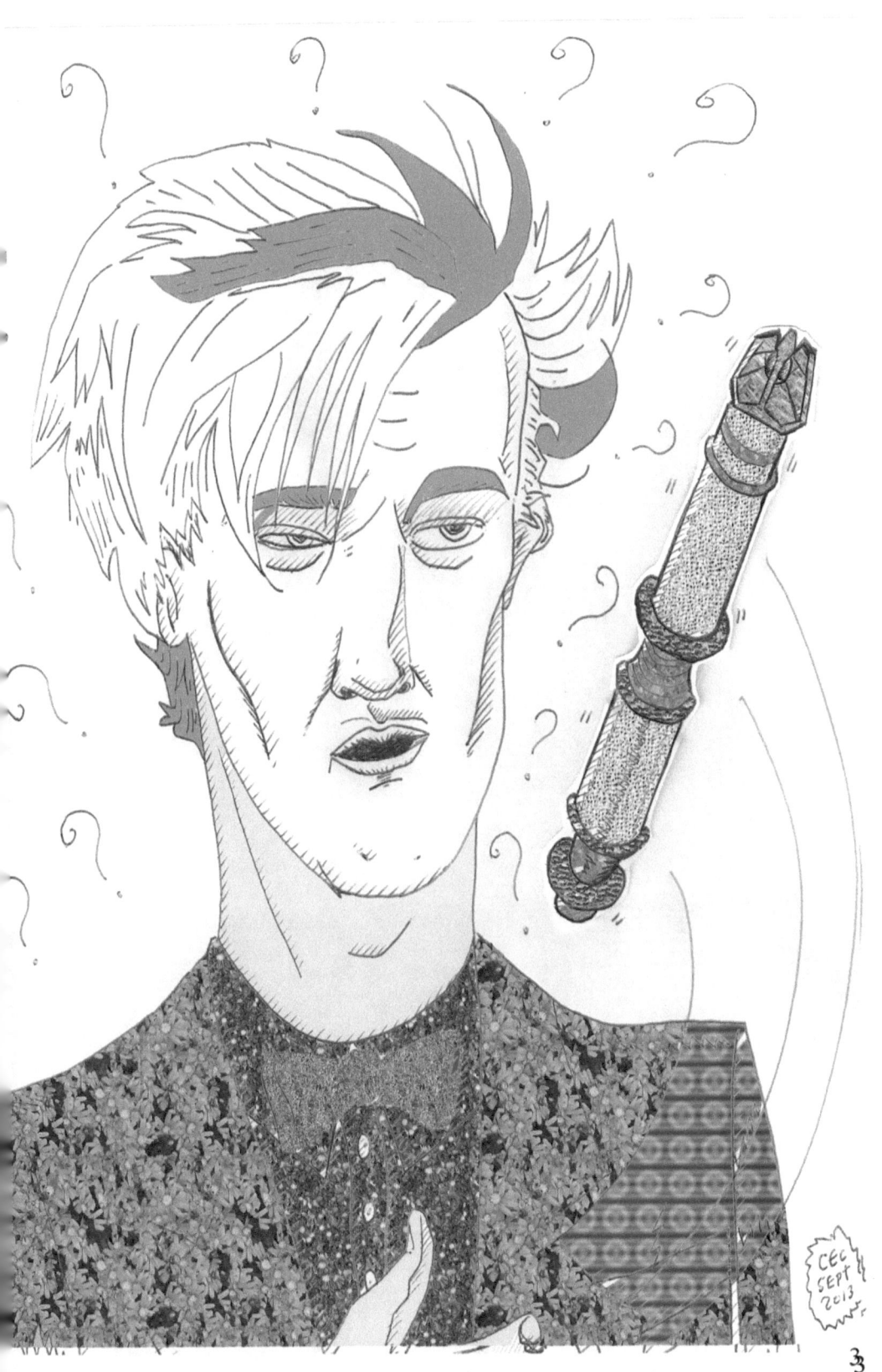

CÉC
SEPT
2013

3

Sketch book, Vol 2:

December 1995 ∞ January 1996

CEC

<(8)>Insomniacs Distribution Cooperation

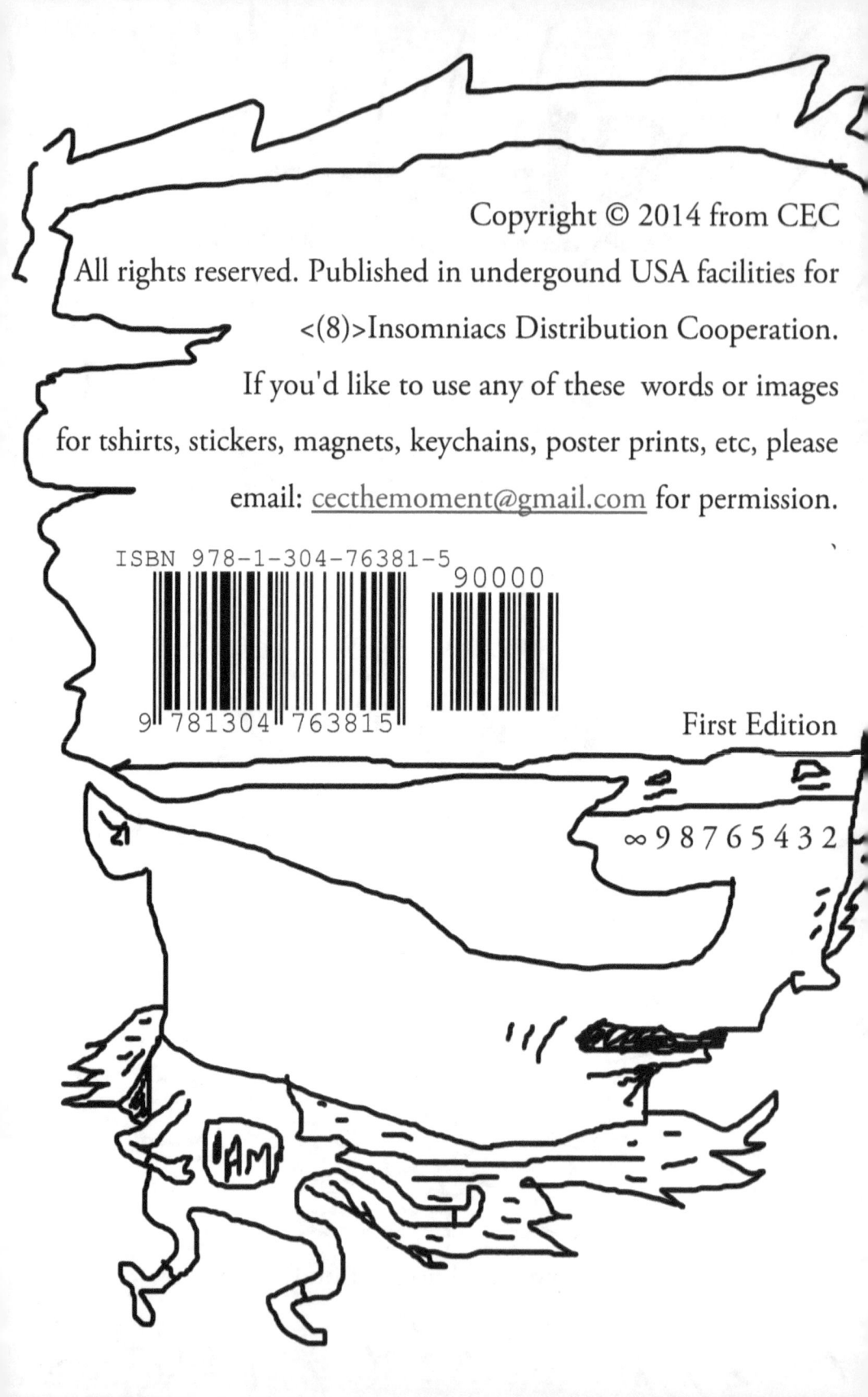

ISBN 978-1-304-76381-5

90000

9 781304 763815

First Edition

∞ 9 8 7 6 5 4 3 2

Thank you for giving
your talents and passions
frequent opportunities to play.

This is dedicated to you
for shining your light so
we could see ours.

King of the mountain

IAM

Introduction

There are 9 volumes of these sketchbooks. They are from when I was still in Columbia College. The idea was to release a new one every couple of months. 2012, I got the first sketchbook sent off to the printers before 2013 rolled around. It is now 11:21pm on New Year's Eve. 10 hours of the Doctor Who Theme Song has been playing for added triumphancy. This is the second volume and ideally will be finished and sent off to printing before 2014. Boy, hatta thrill! Look to the billboards for what's been going on over the past year. The seeds have been planted, growing, and millimoments away from exploding through like colonies of bamboo forests. You have contributed to this and we all thank you dearly for it!

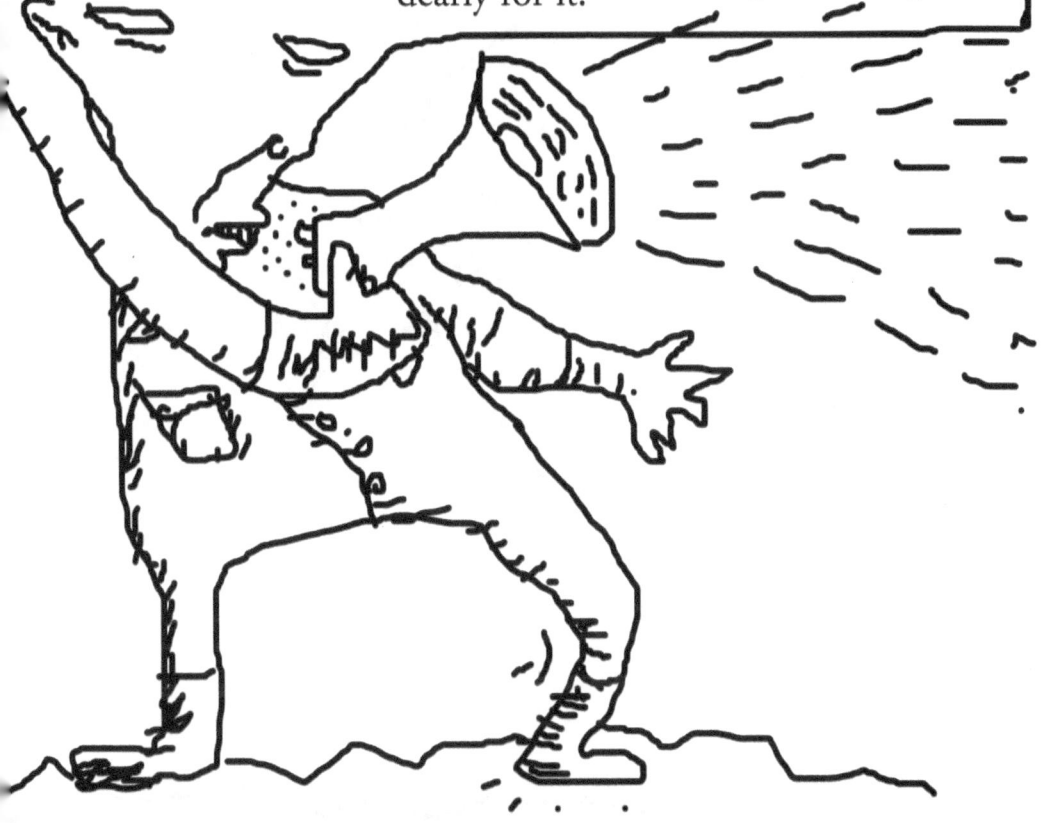

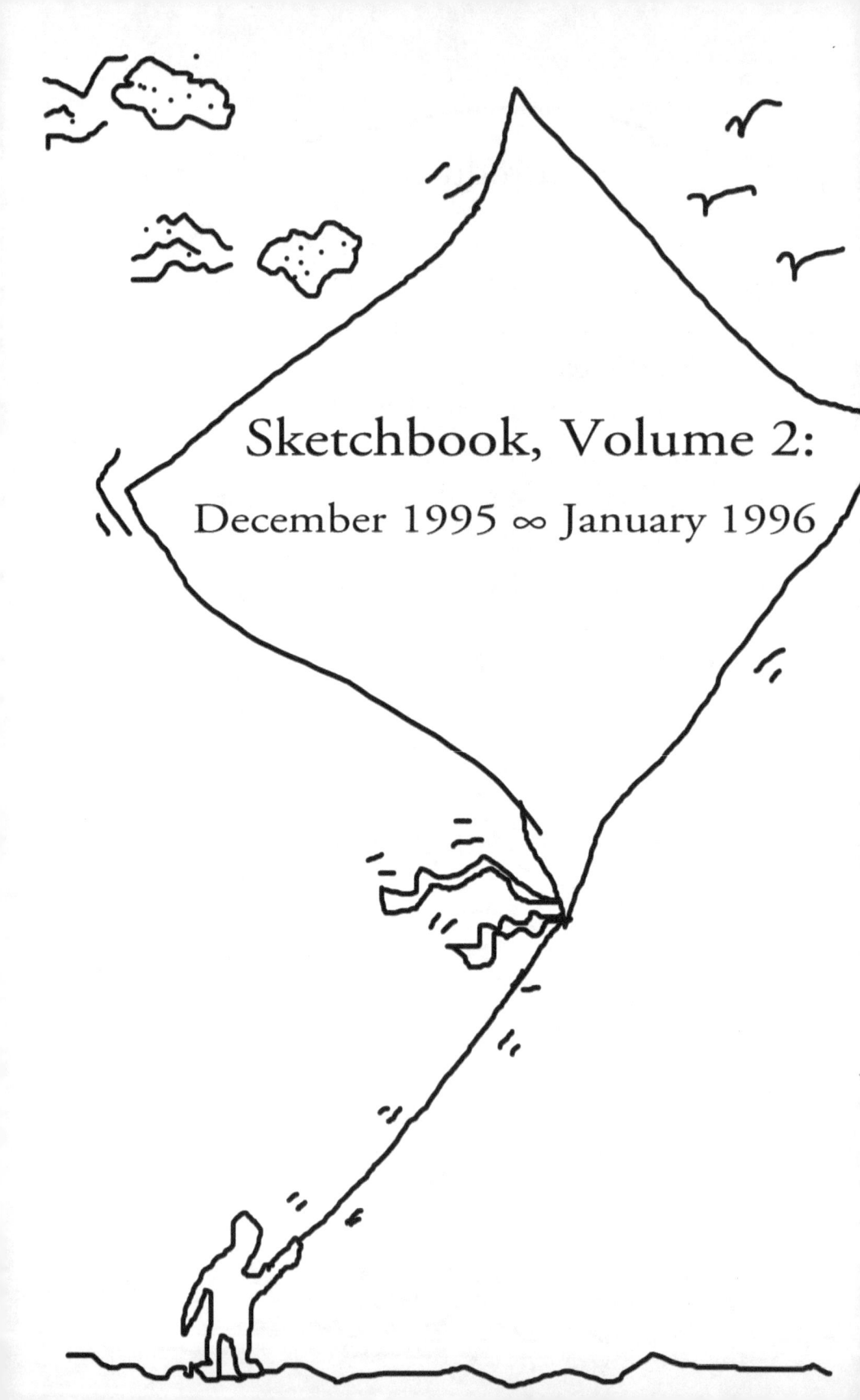

Sketchbook, Volume 2:

December 1995 ∞ January 1996

me

An extremely durable, heavyweight (80#) sketching paper
Designed for versatile use indoors or out
For pencil, ink, pastel, color markers, and watercolor
Bound with heavy paperboard backing for support and safekeeping

70 s
9 x 6 i

C   É   C

Sketch
Diary

The Me   Corporation, DiMension   5   U S S U

CURT CLENDENIN 12/25/95

Curt Clendenin ©

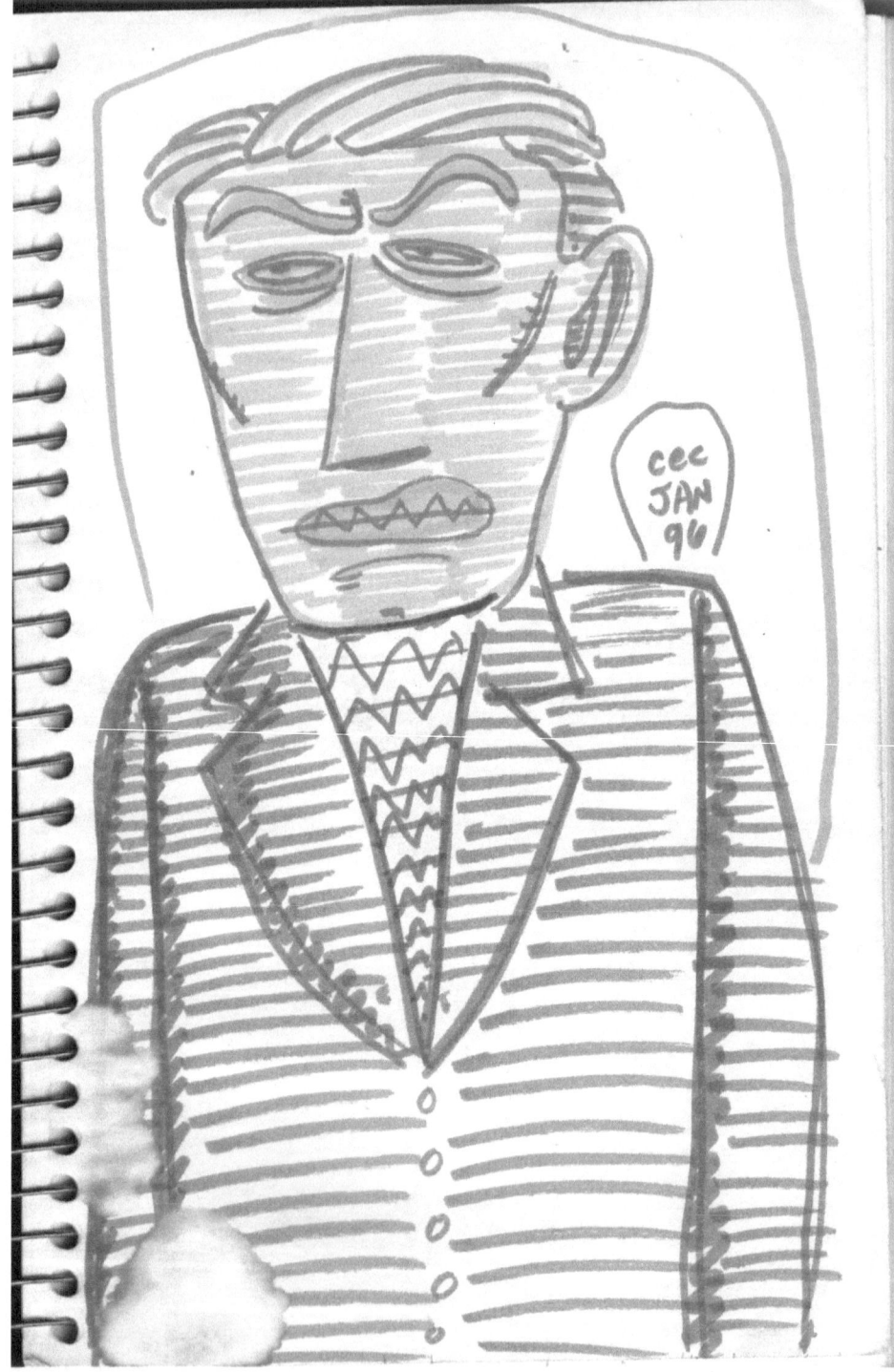

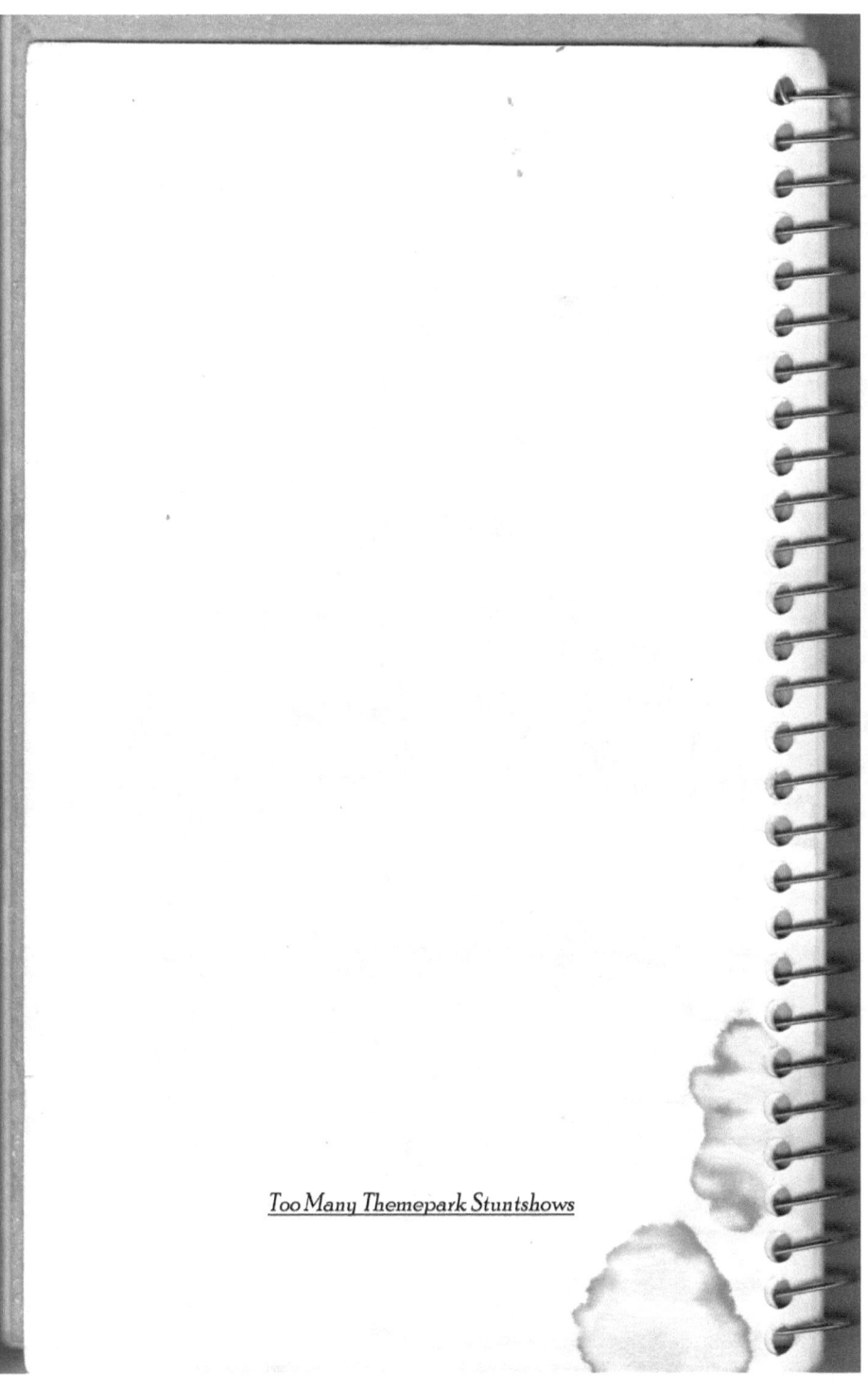

Too Many Themepark Stuntshows

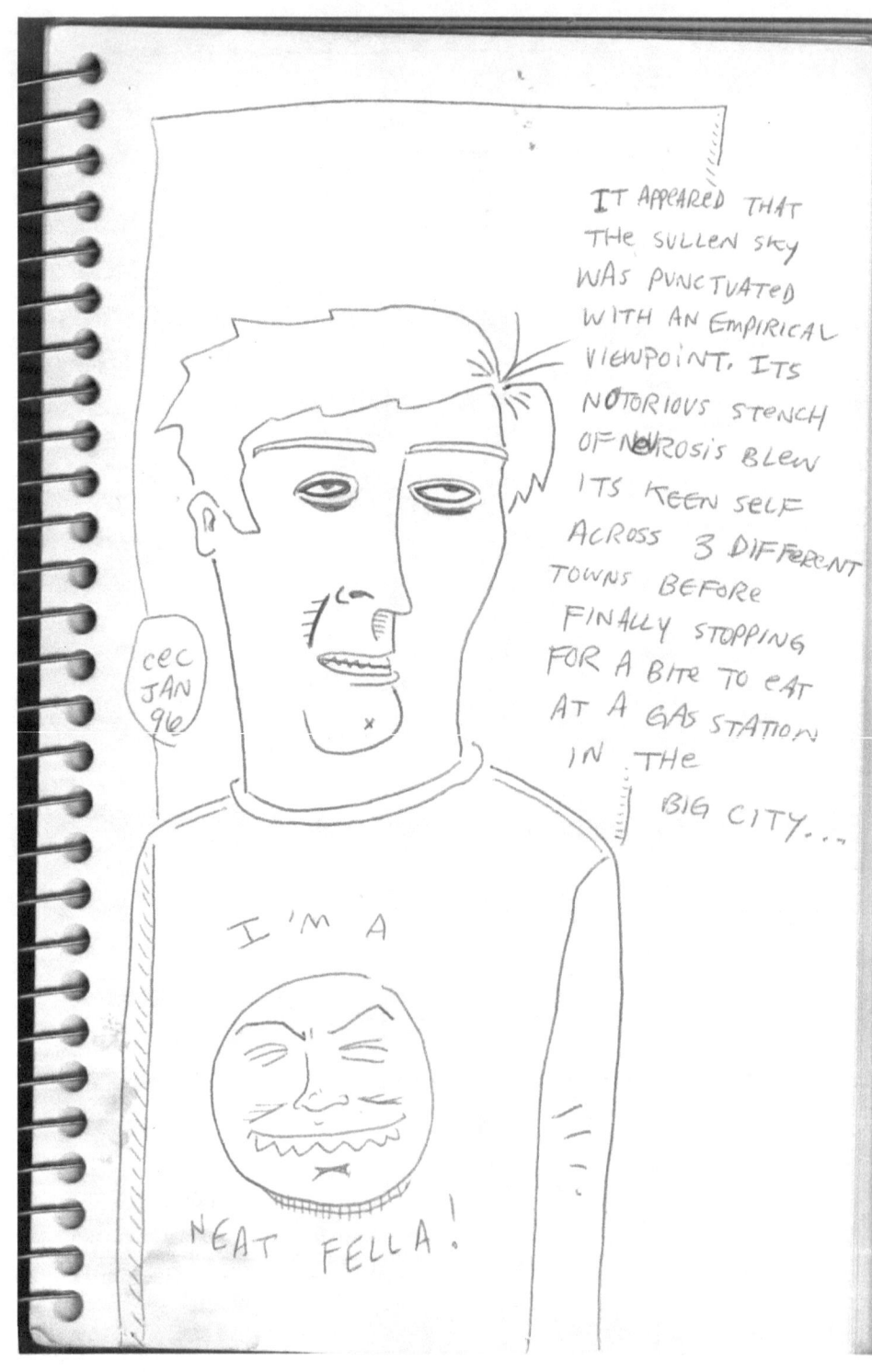

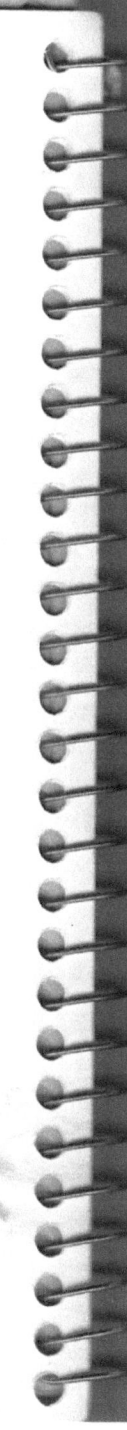

In a racing

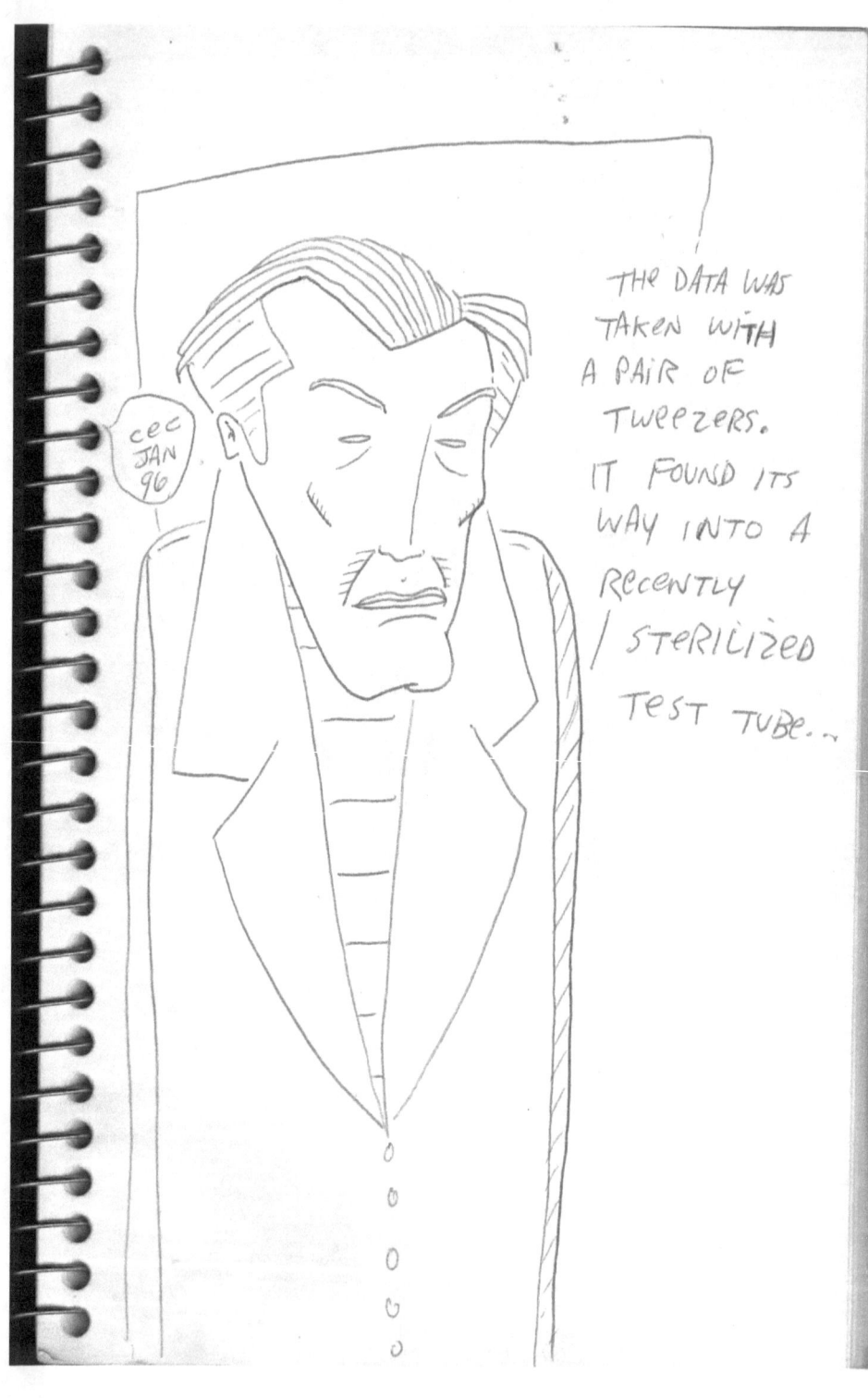

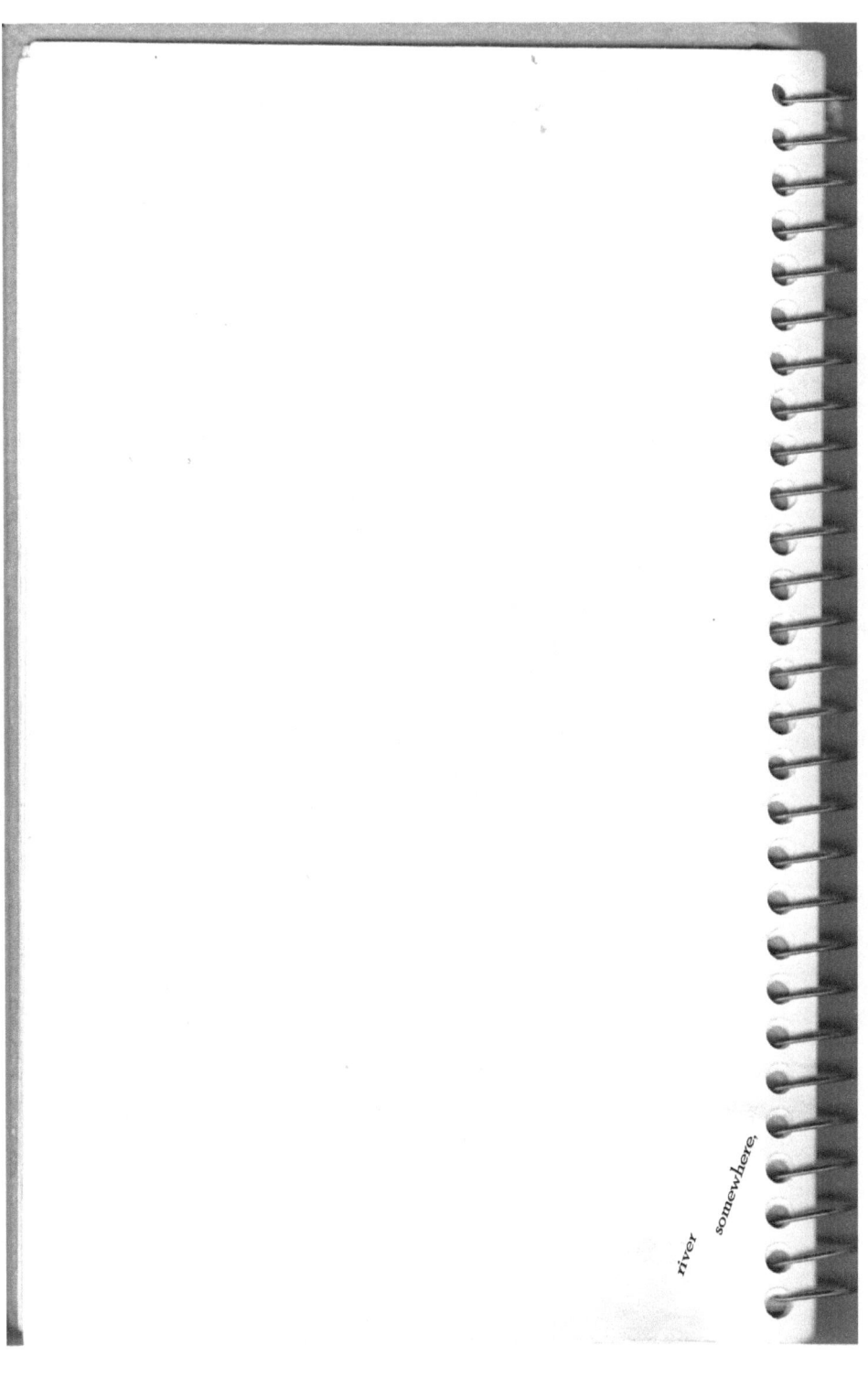

river   somewhere,

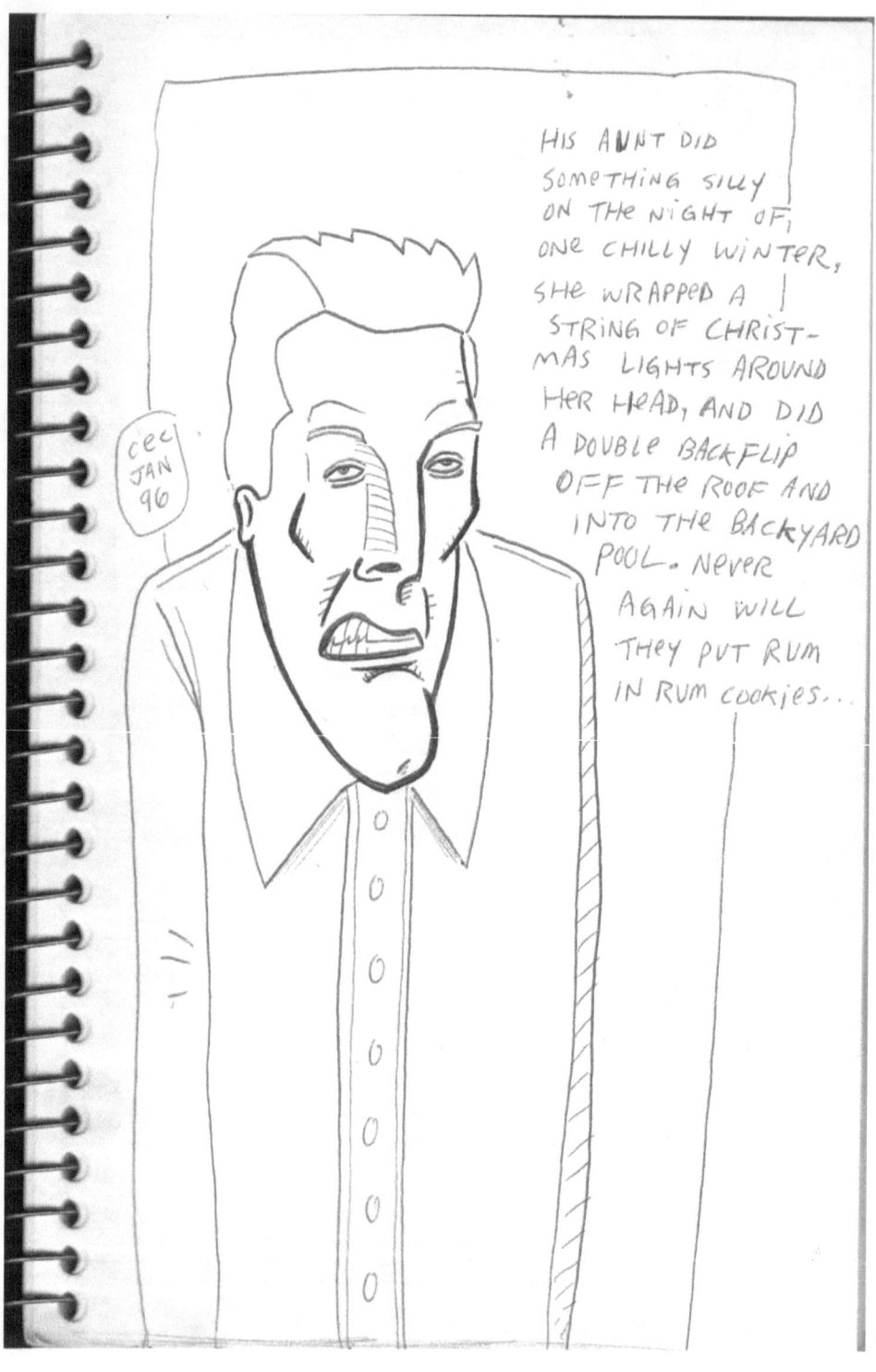

a man

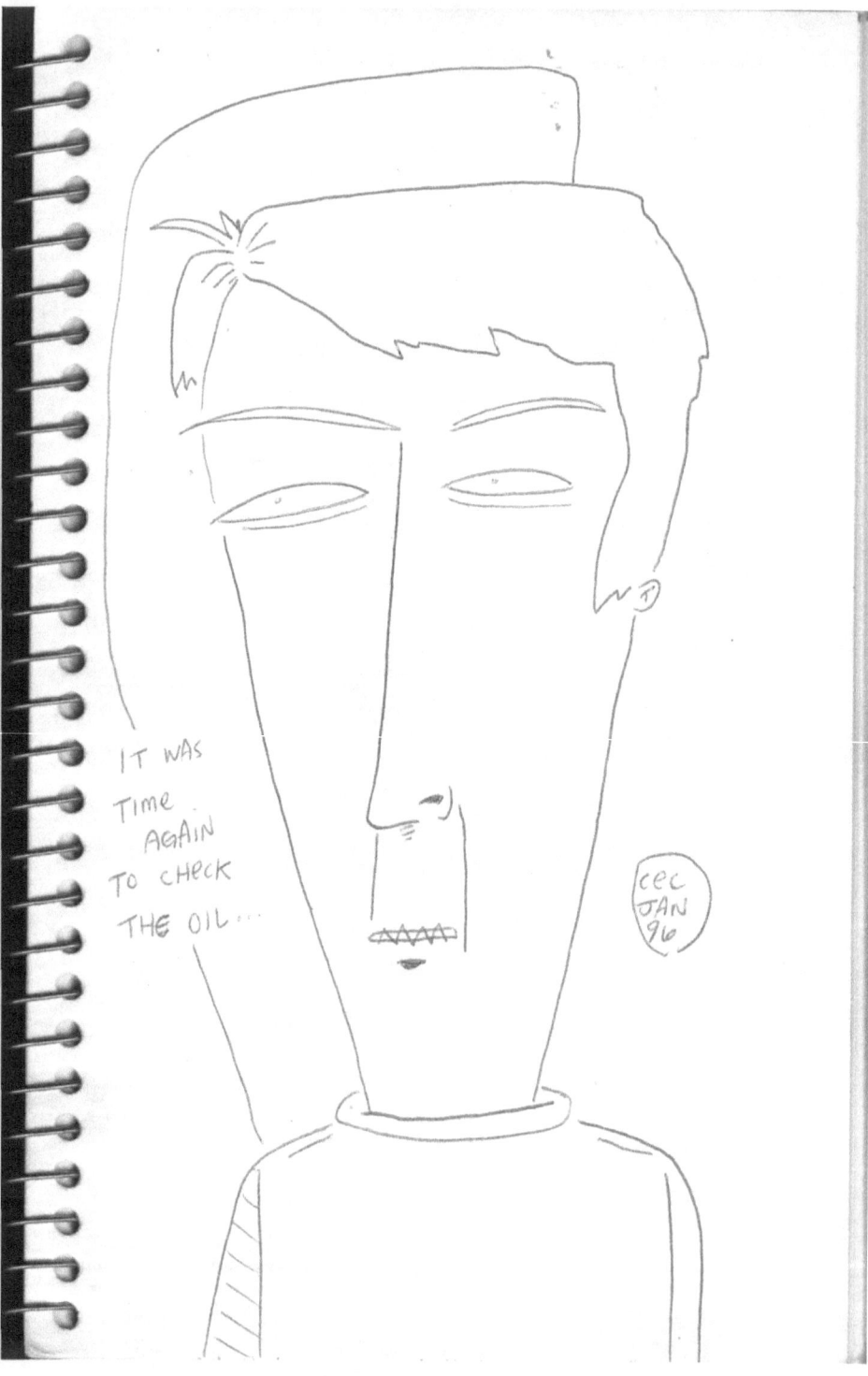

is trapped

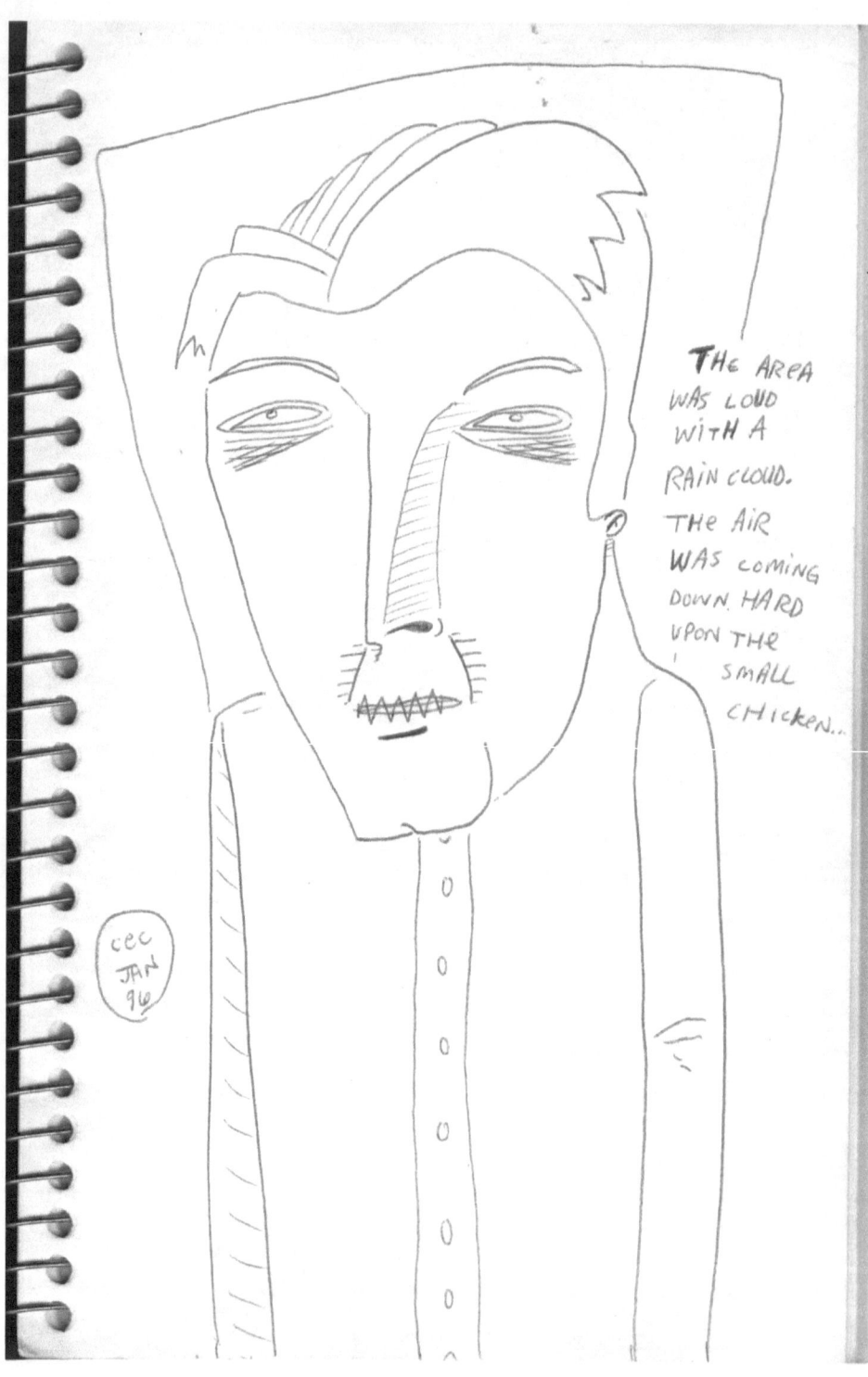

THE AREA
WAS LOUD
WITH A
RAIN CLOUD.
THE AIR
WAS COMING
DOWN. HARD
UPON THE
SMALL
CHICKEN...

in an

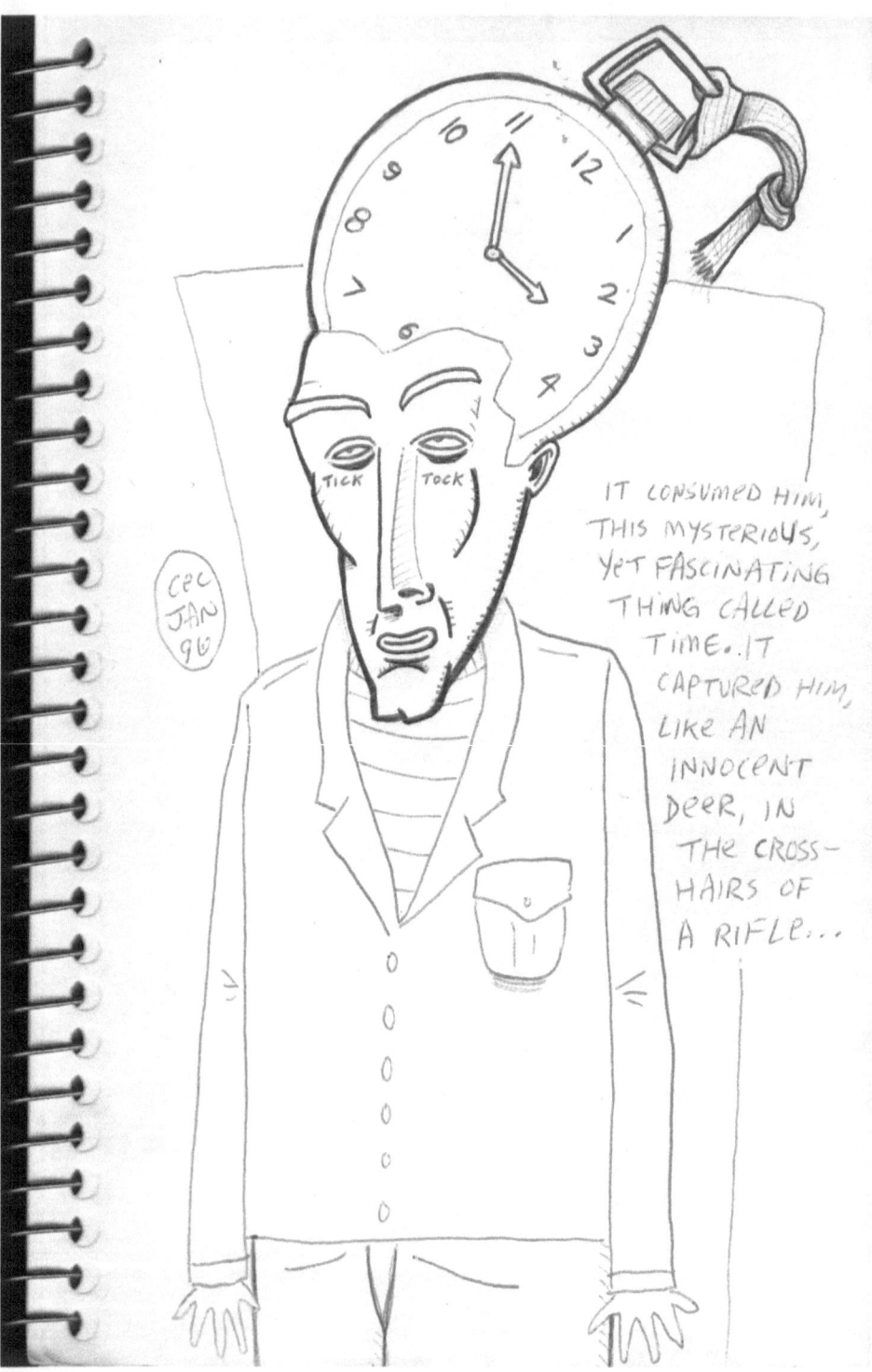

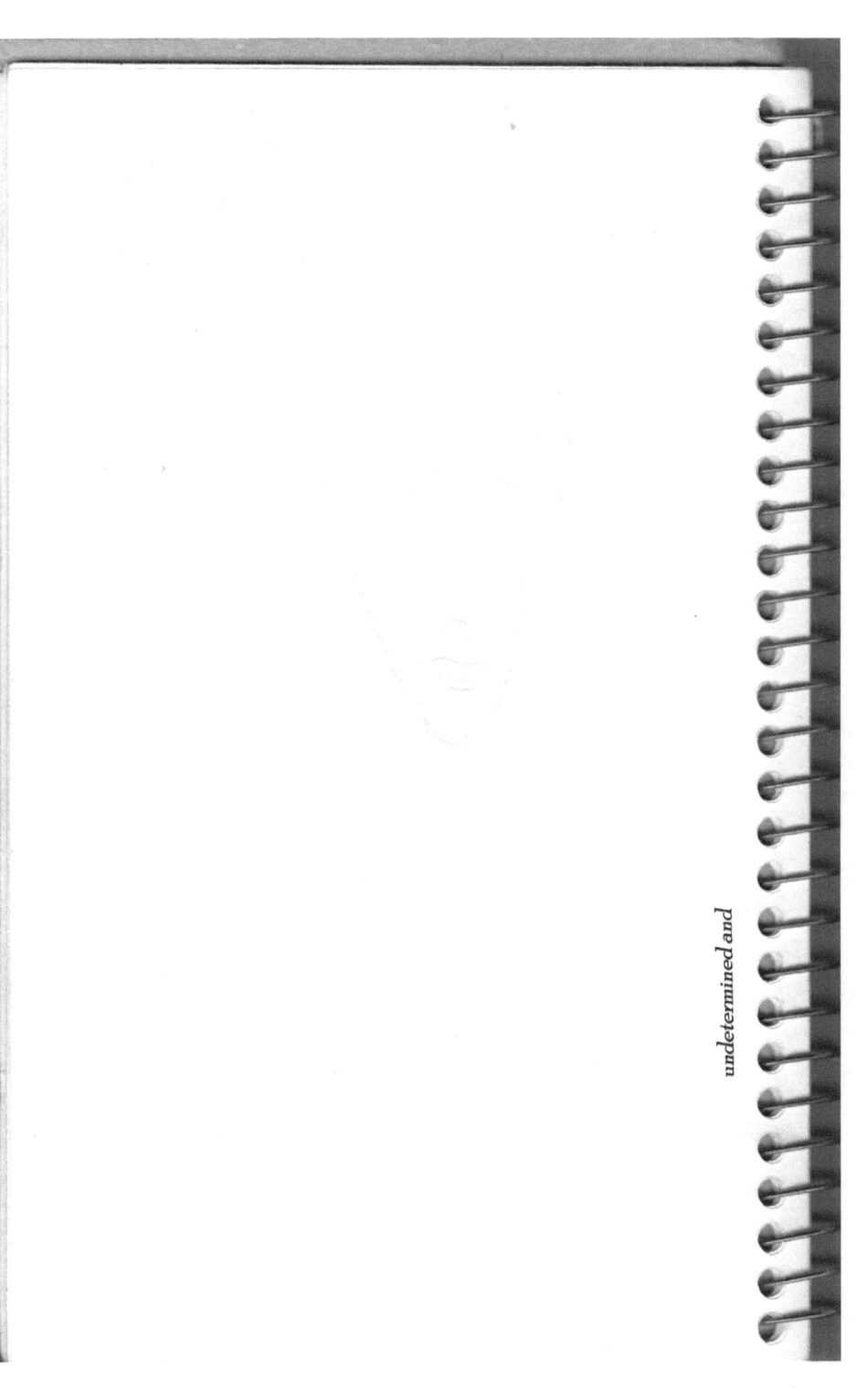

undetermined and

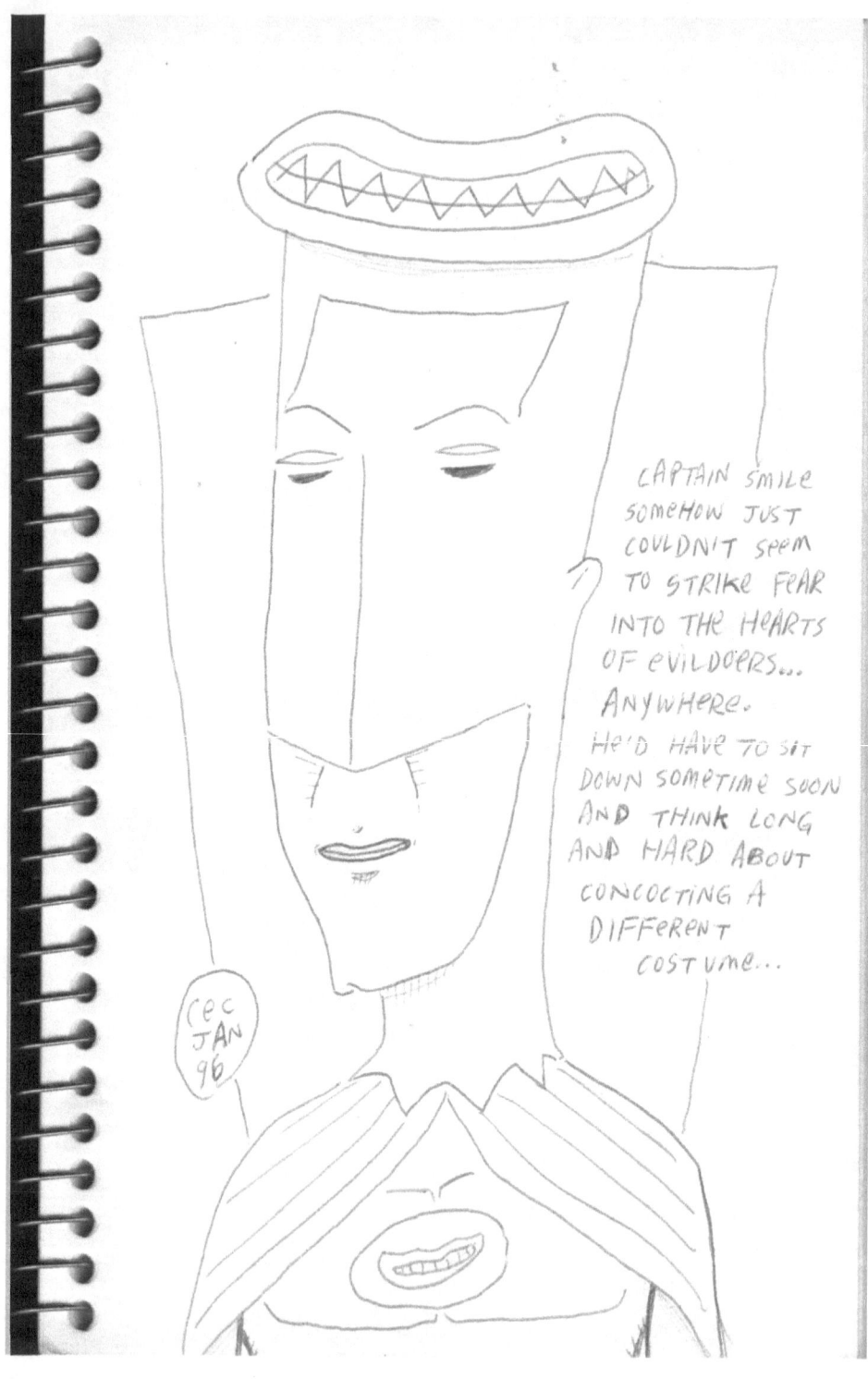

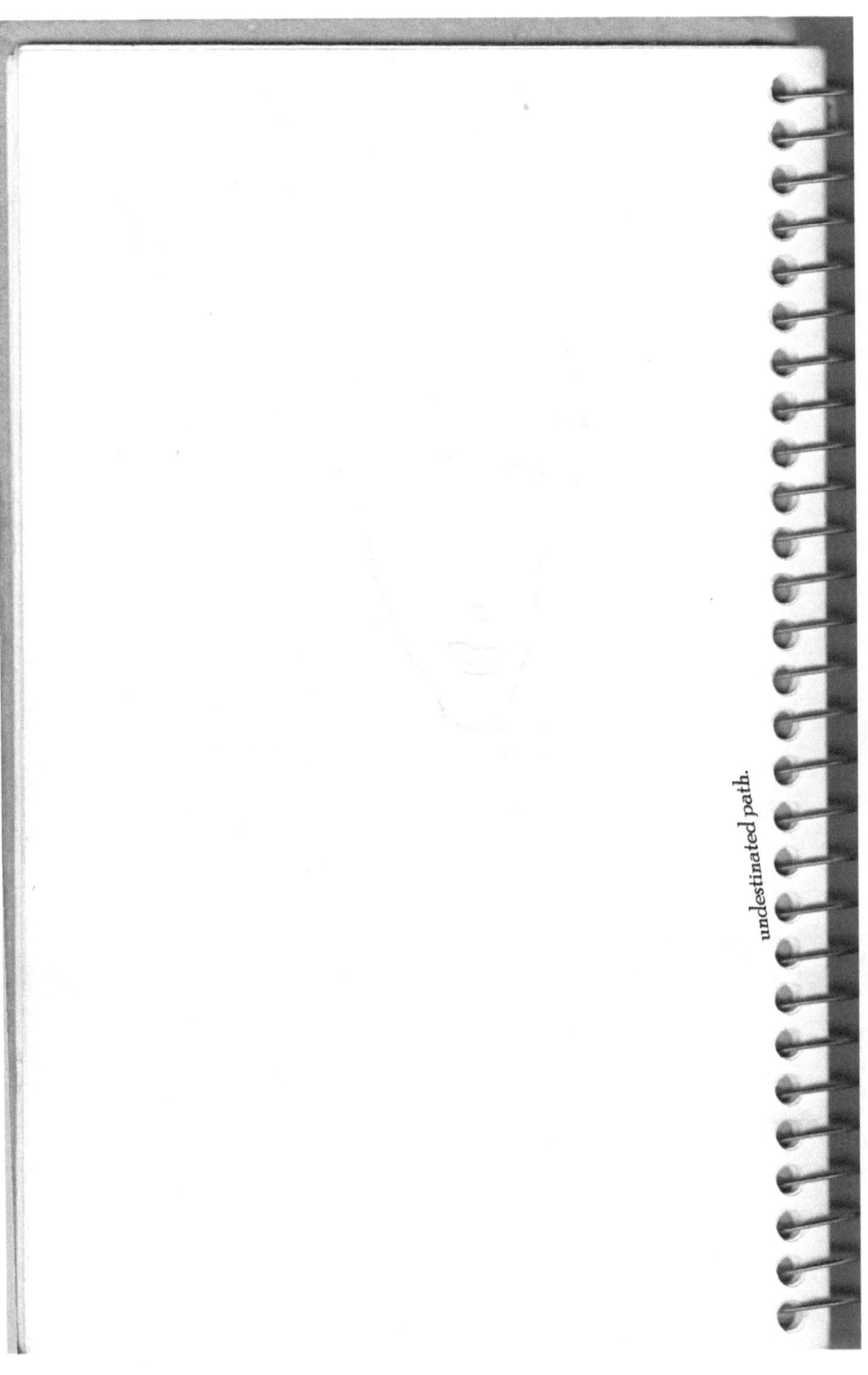

undestinated path.

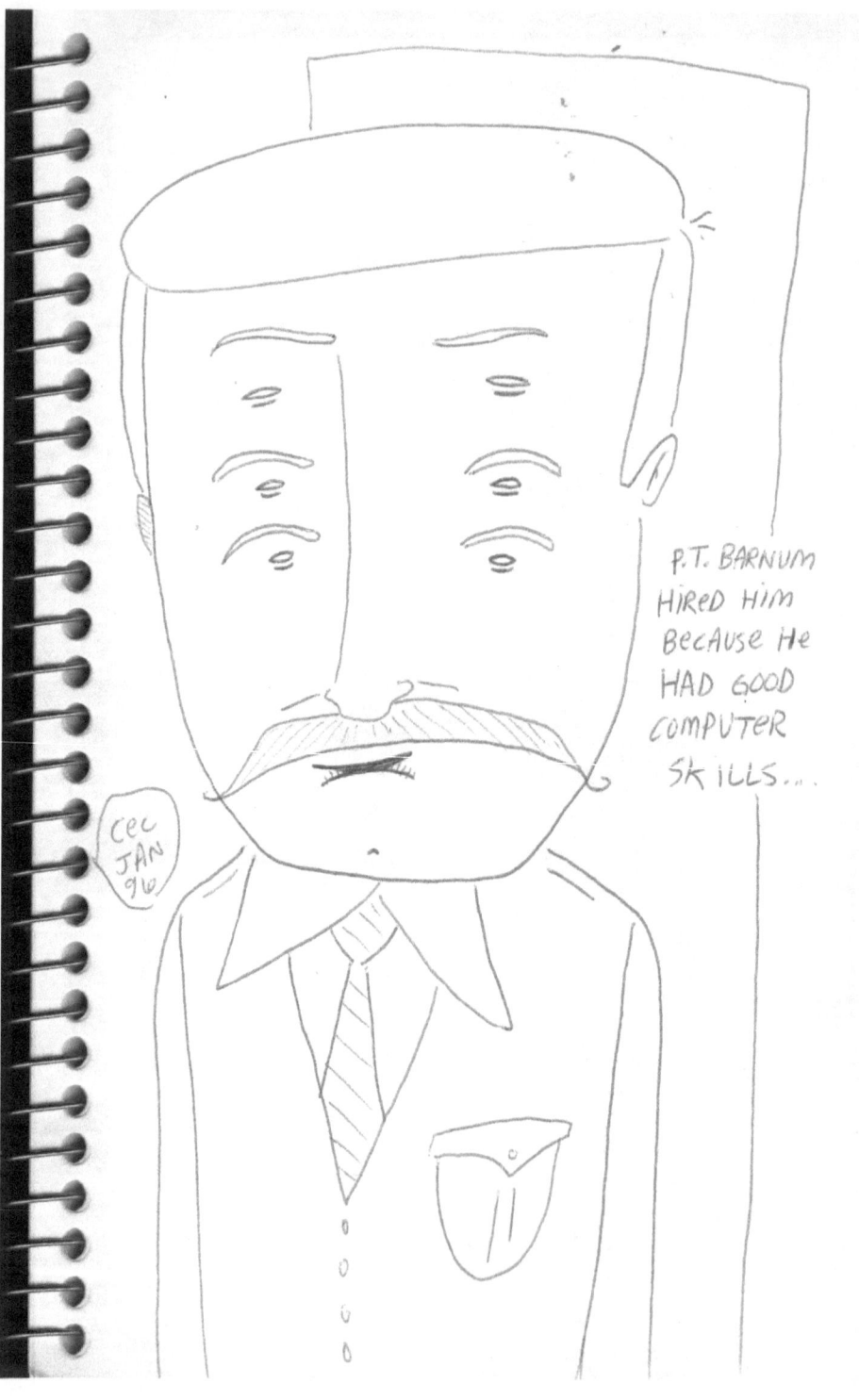

To anyone watching,

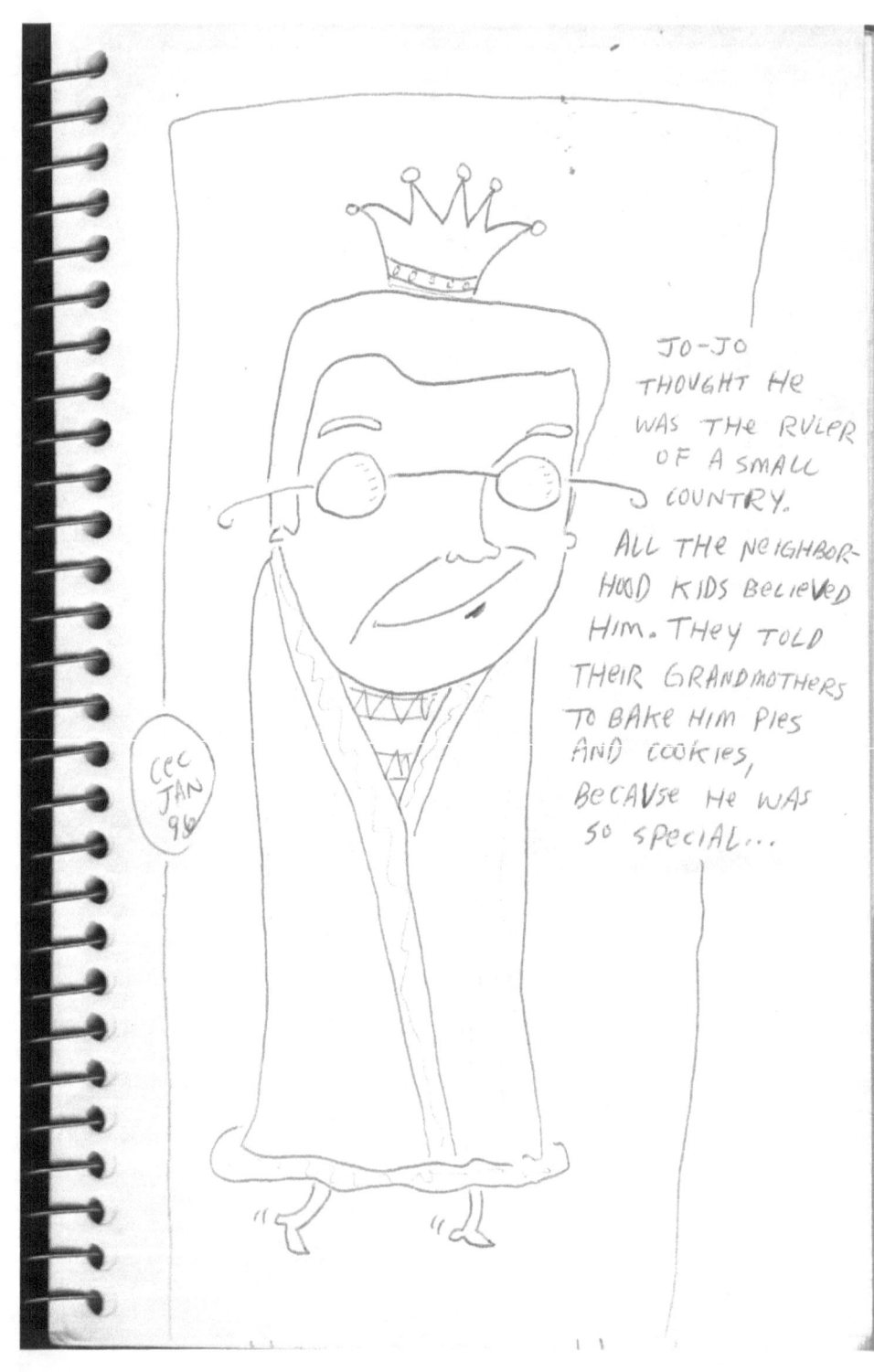

JO-JO THOUGHT HE WAS THE RULER OF A SMALL COUNTRY. ALL THE NEIGHBOR-HOOD KIDS BELIEVED HIM. THEY TOLD THEIR GRANDMOTHERS TO BAKE HIM PIES AND COOKIES, BECAUSE HE WAS SO SPECIAL...

it might

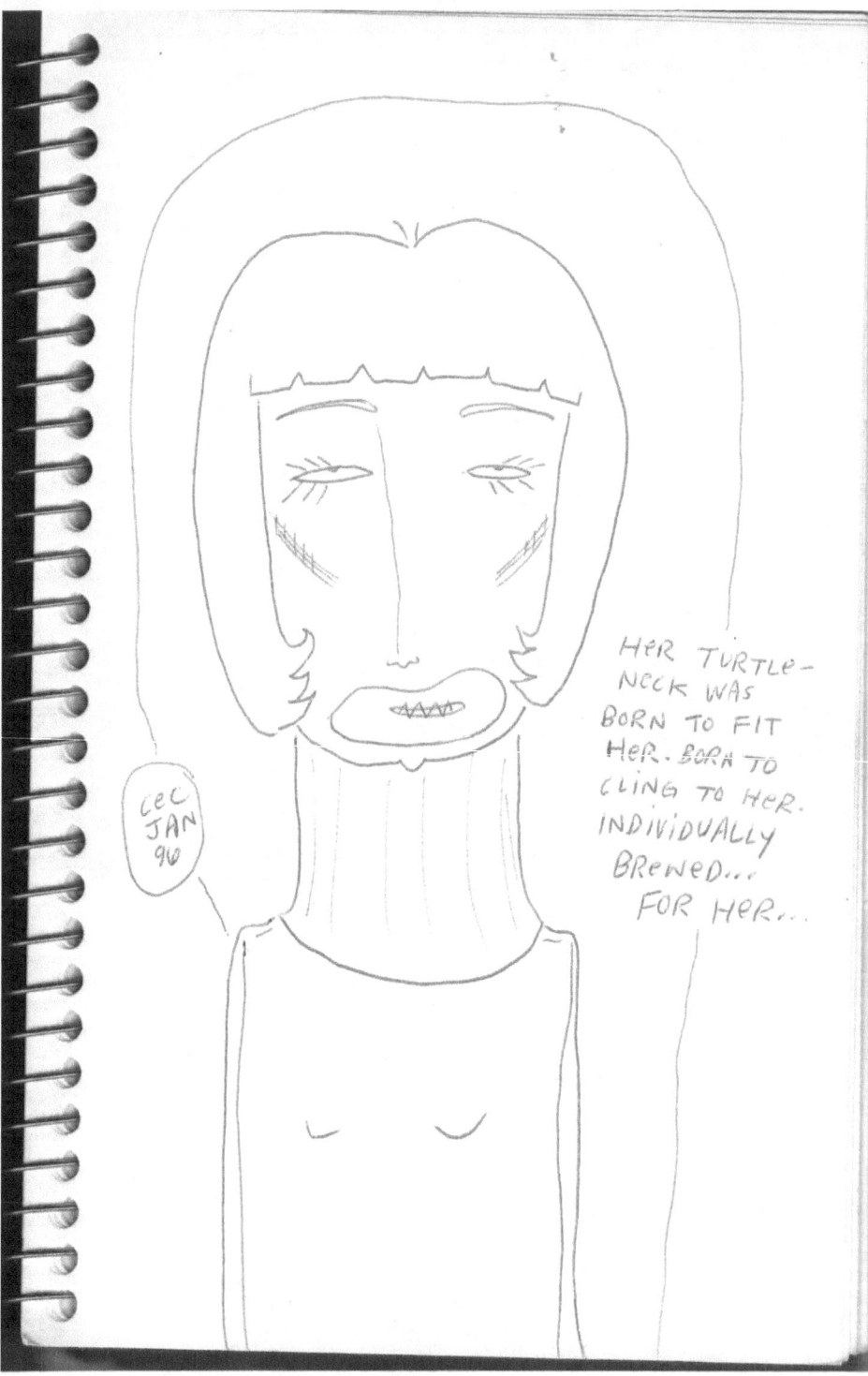

look like

THE PAPER, IN ALL ITS
MAGNIFICENT SPLENDOR,
WAS WHITE. IT CREATED
WORLDS, THOUGHTS, REALMS...
JUST BY BEING WHAT IT
WAS. WHITE. A NET
WITH A GREAT MANY
HANDFULLS OF POSSIBILITIES...

CEC
JAN
96

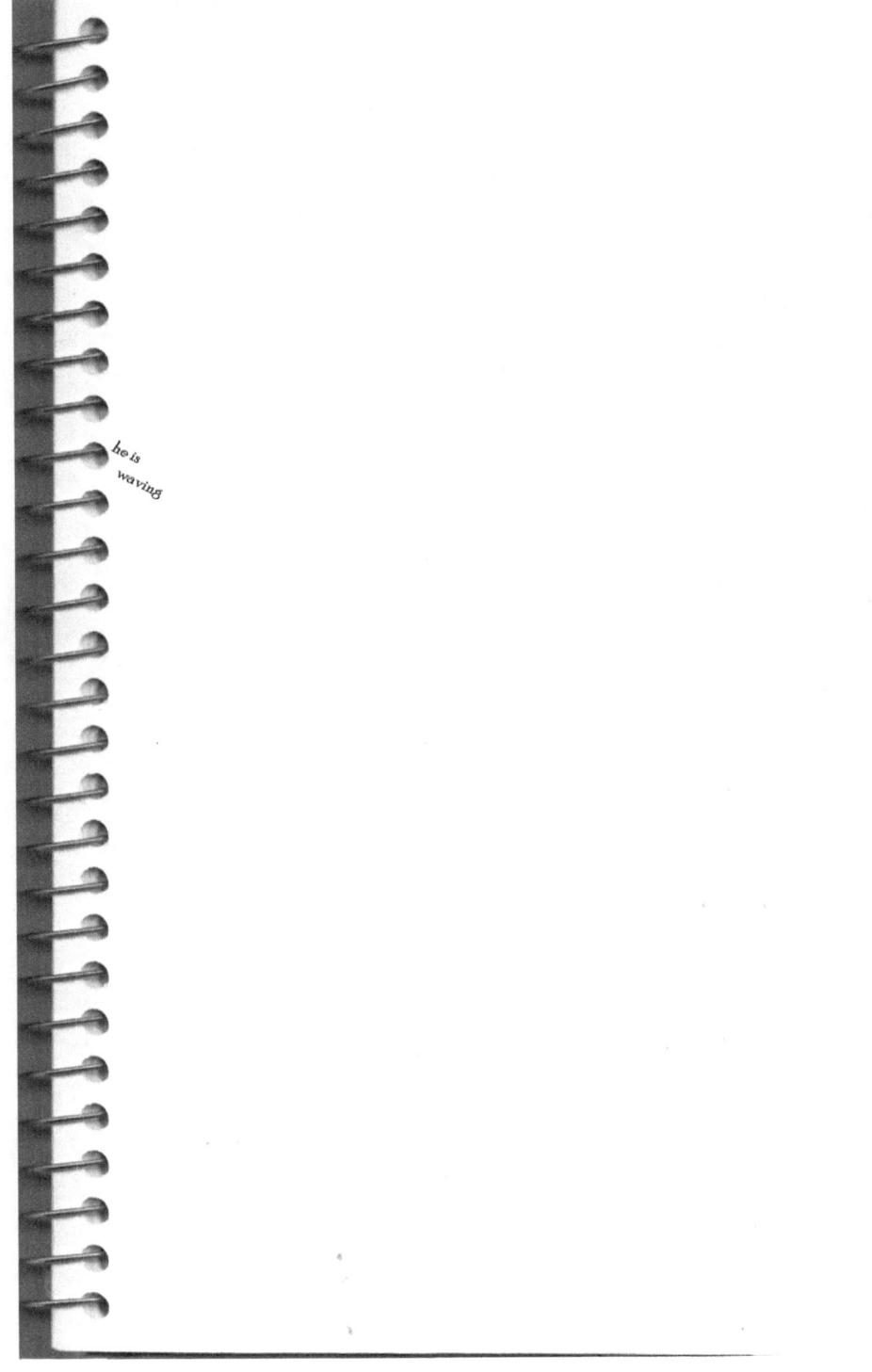

he is
waving

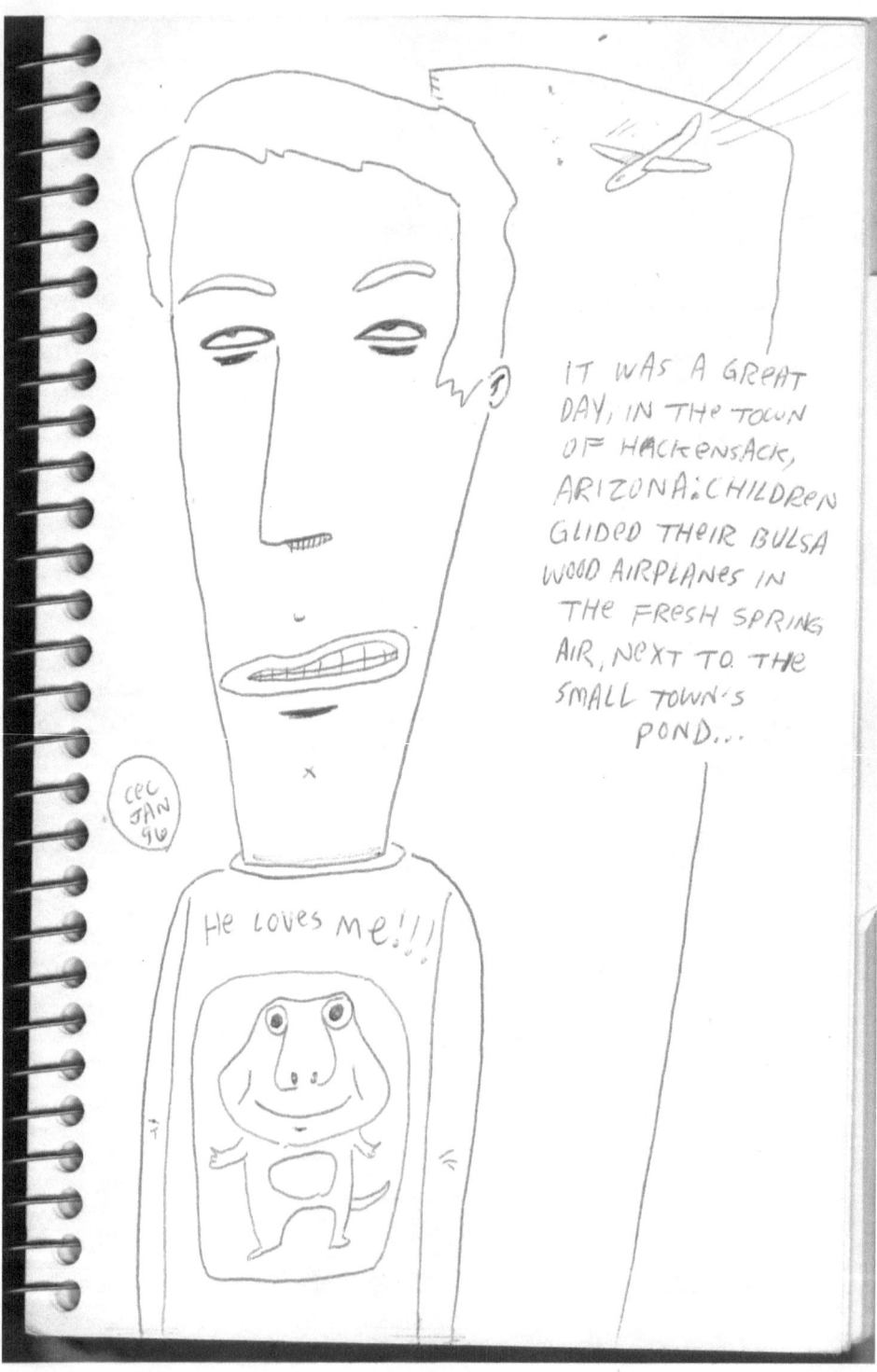

IT WAS A GREAT DAY, IN THE TOWN OF HACKENSACK, ARIZONA: CHILDREN GLIDED THEIR BULSA WOOD AIRPLANES IN THE FRESH SPRING AIR, NEXT TO THE SMALL TOWN'S POND...

He Loves me!!!

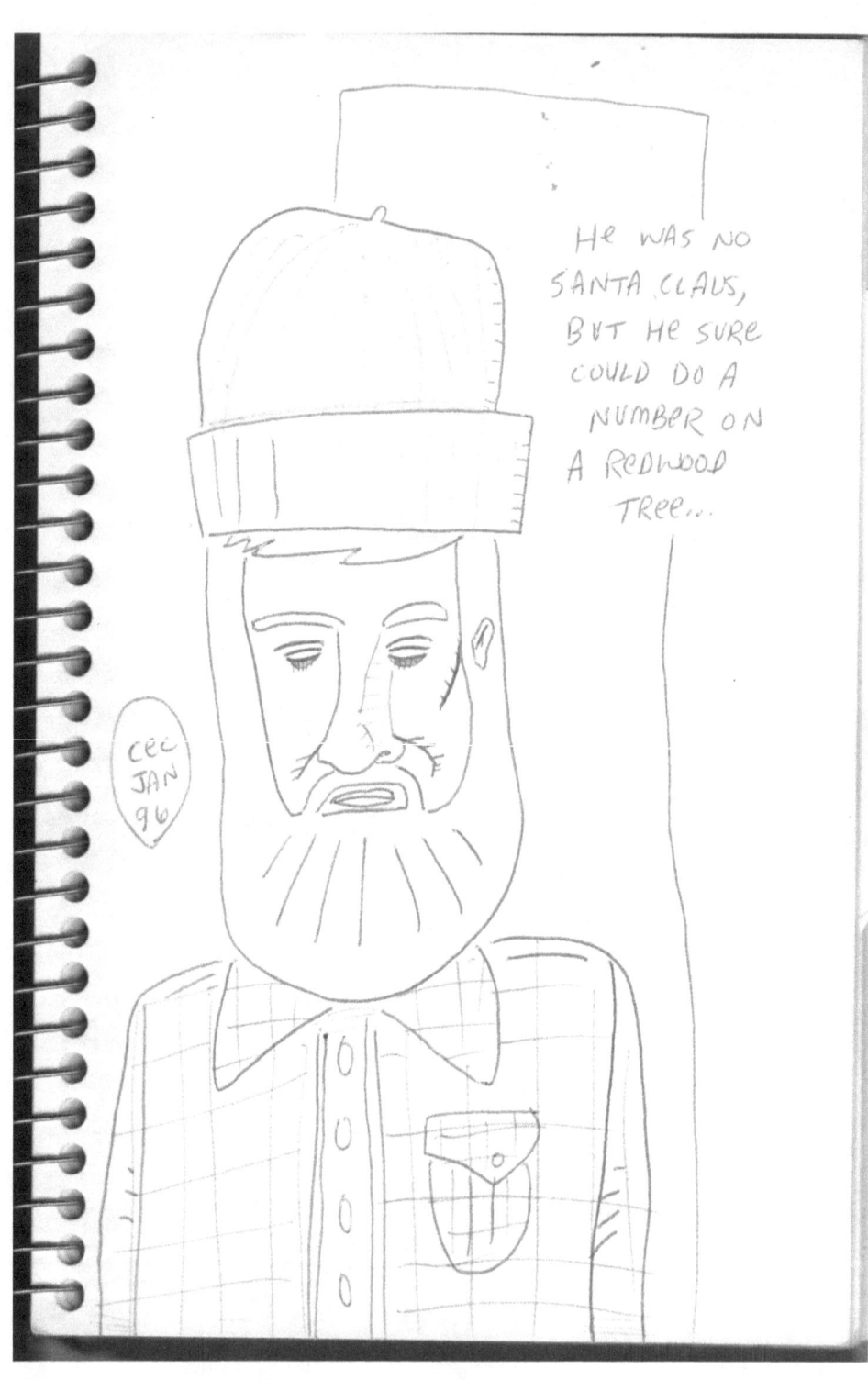

faraway
friend.

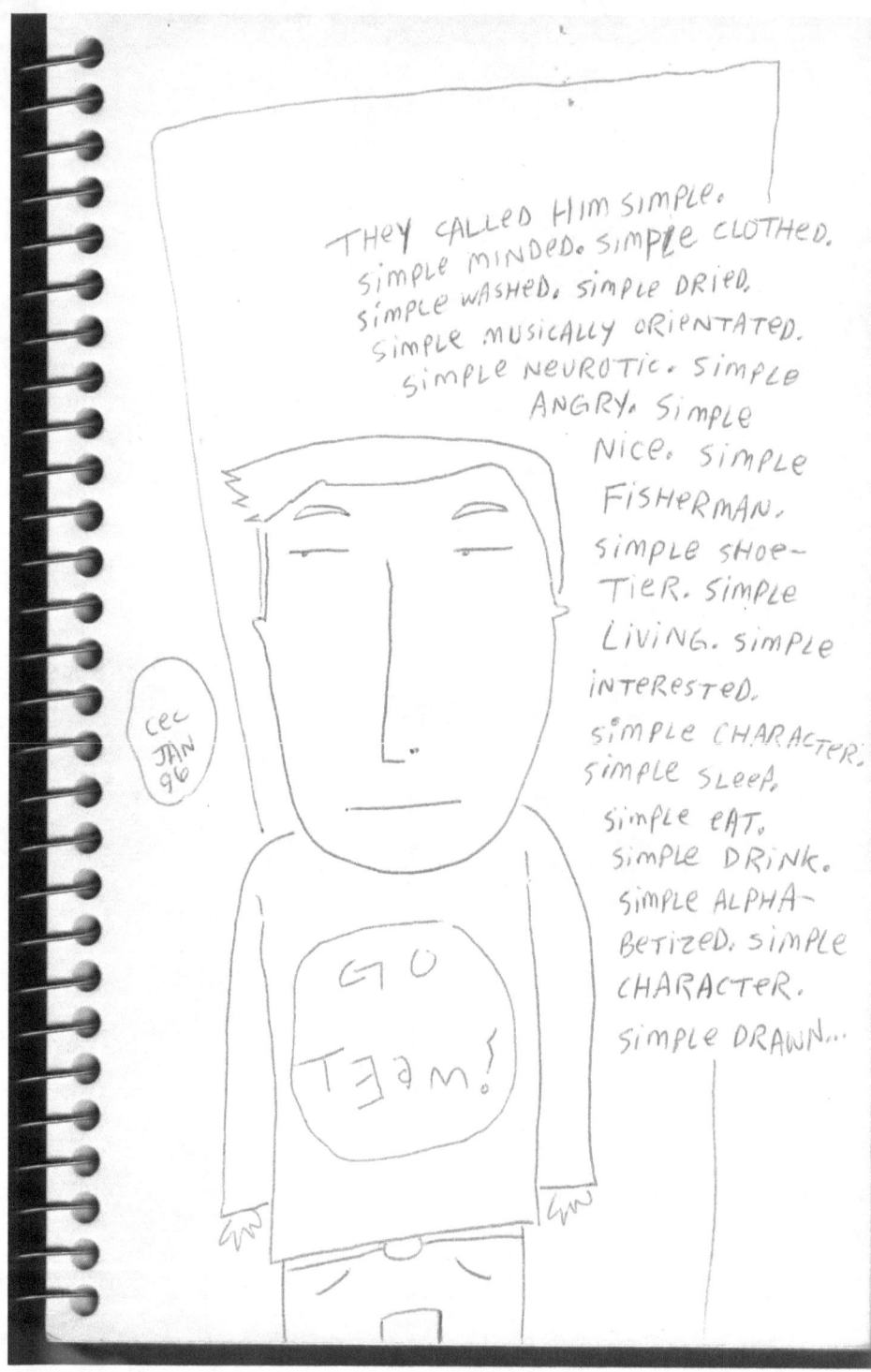

If you

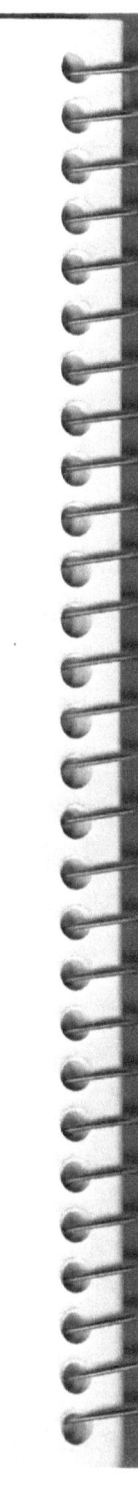

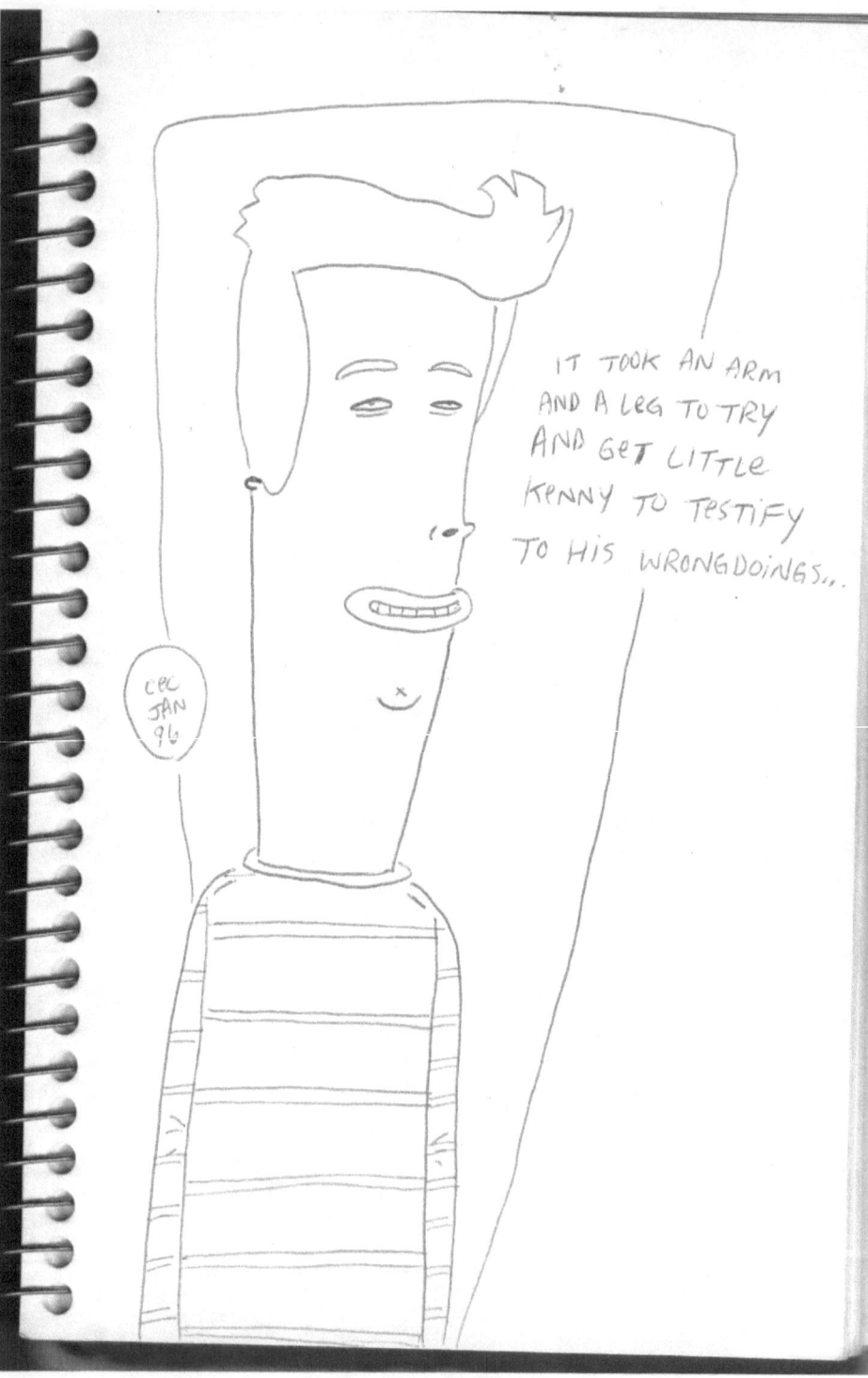

were him,

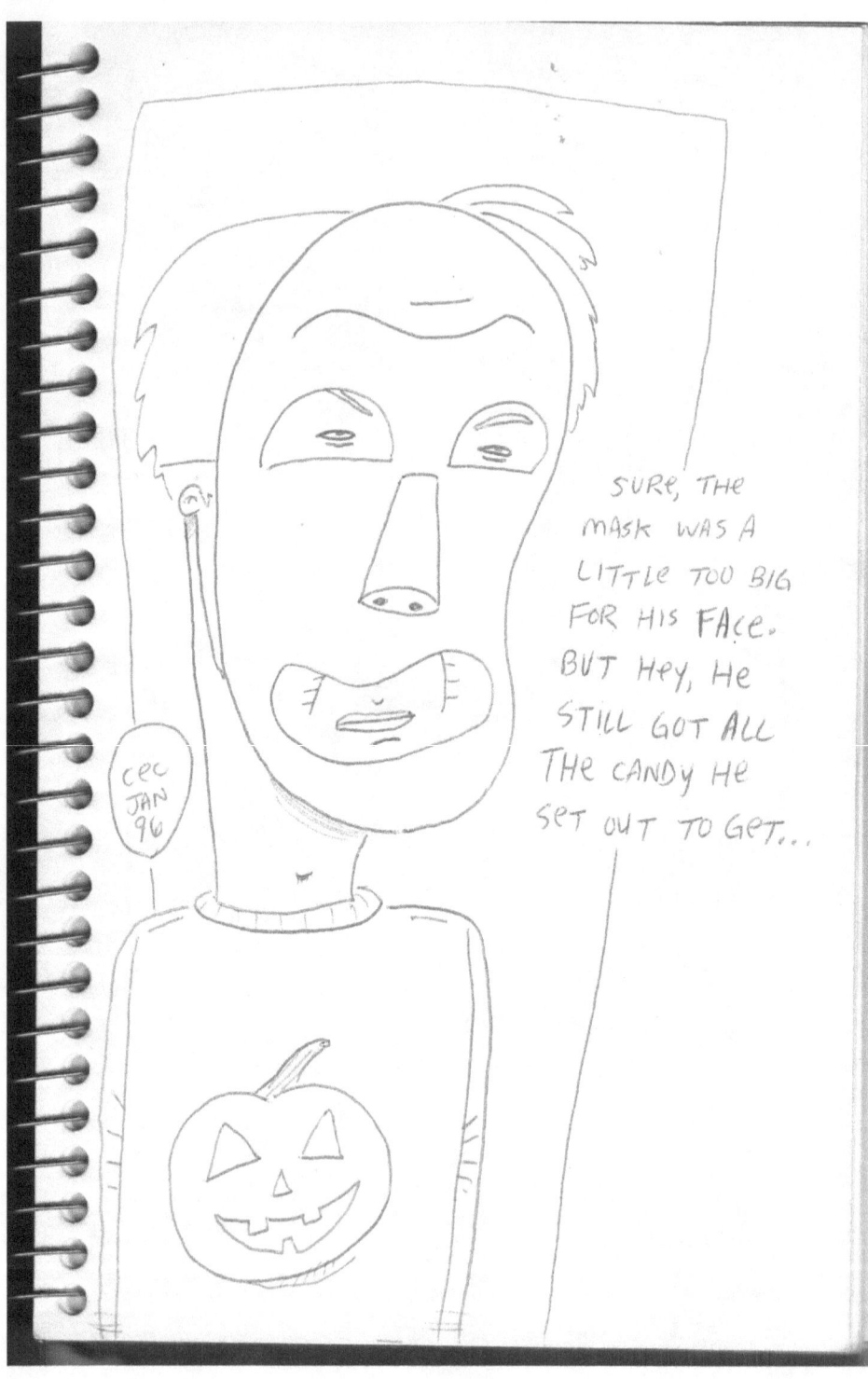

you might

HIS UNCLE
FABRICATED
HIS OWN
CANDLES
ON THE
WEEKENDS.

think you

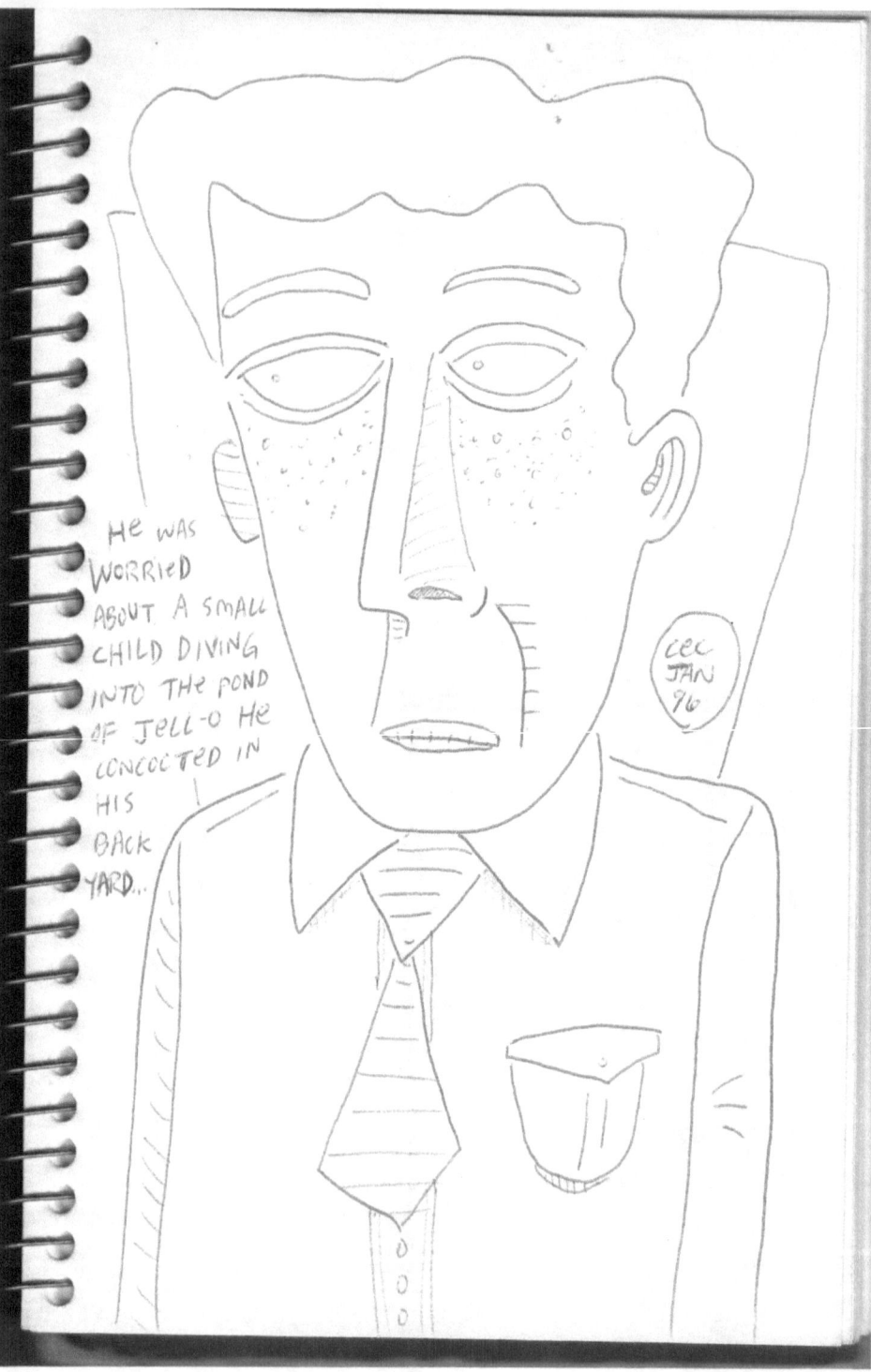

were trying

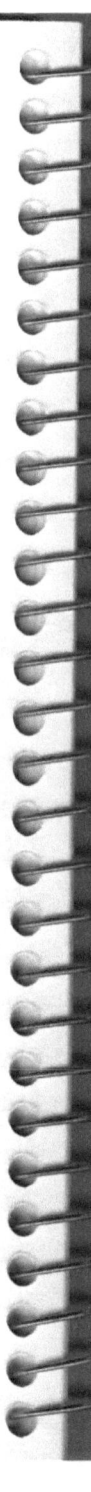

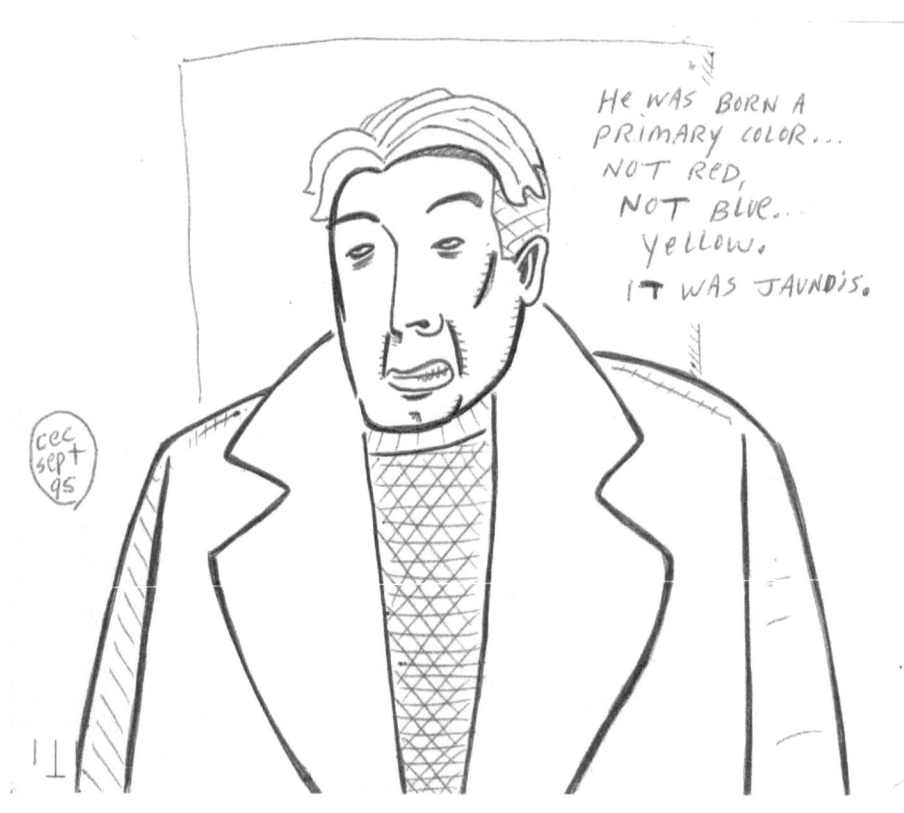

to grab

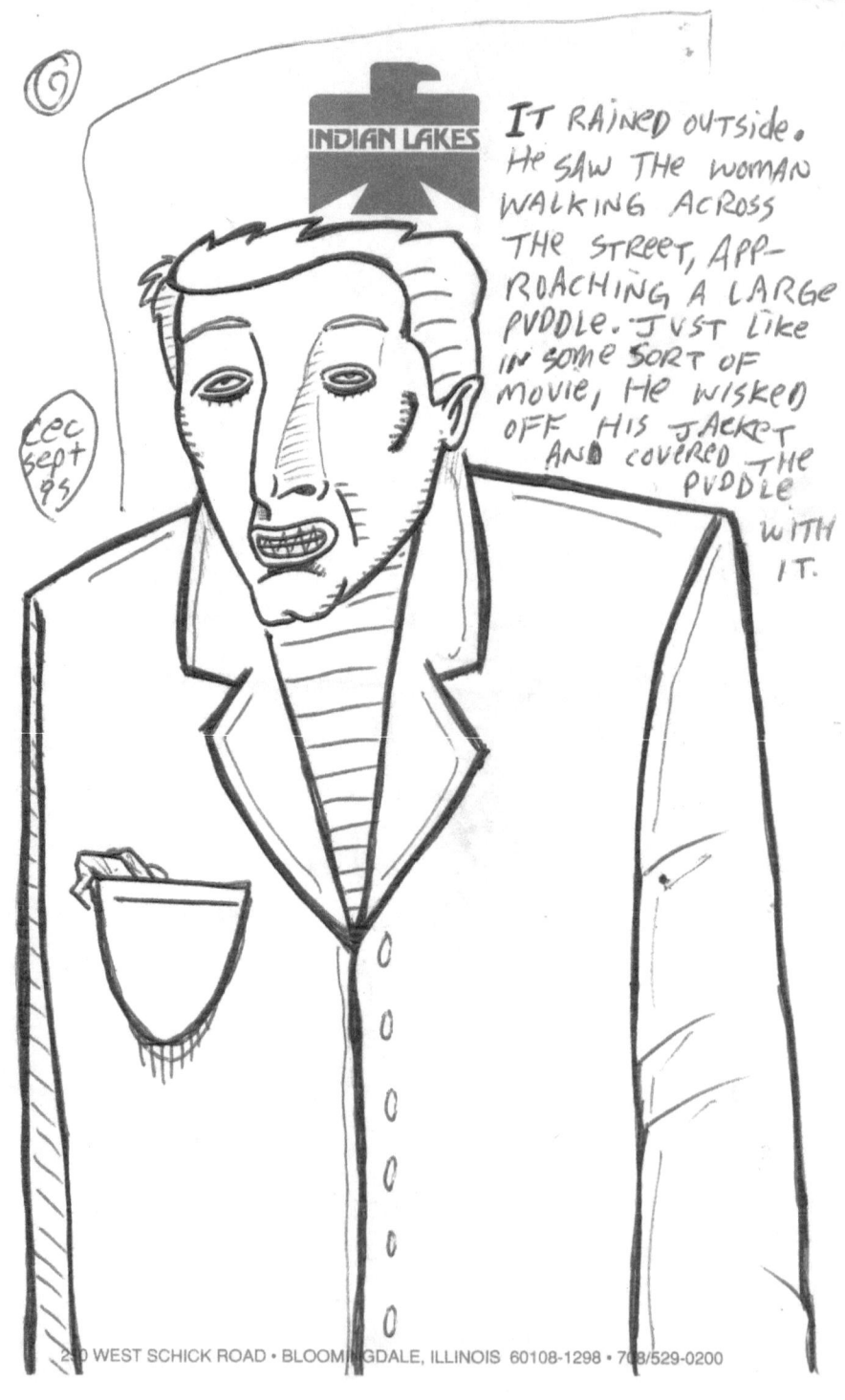

IT RAINED OUTSIDE. He SAW THE WOMAN WALKING ACROSS THE STREET, APPROACHING A LARGE PUDDLE. JUST LIKE IN SOME SORT OF MOVIE, He WISKED OFF HIS JACKET AND COVERED THE PUDDLE WITH IT.

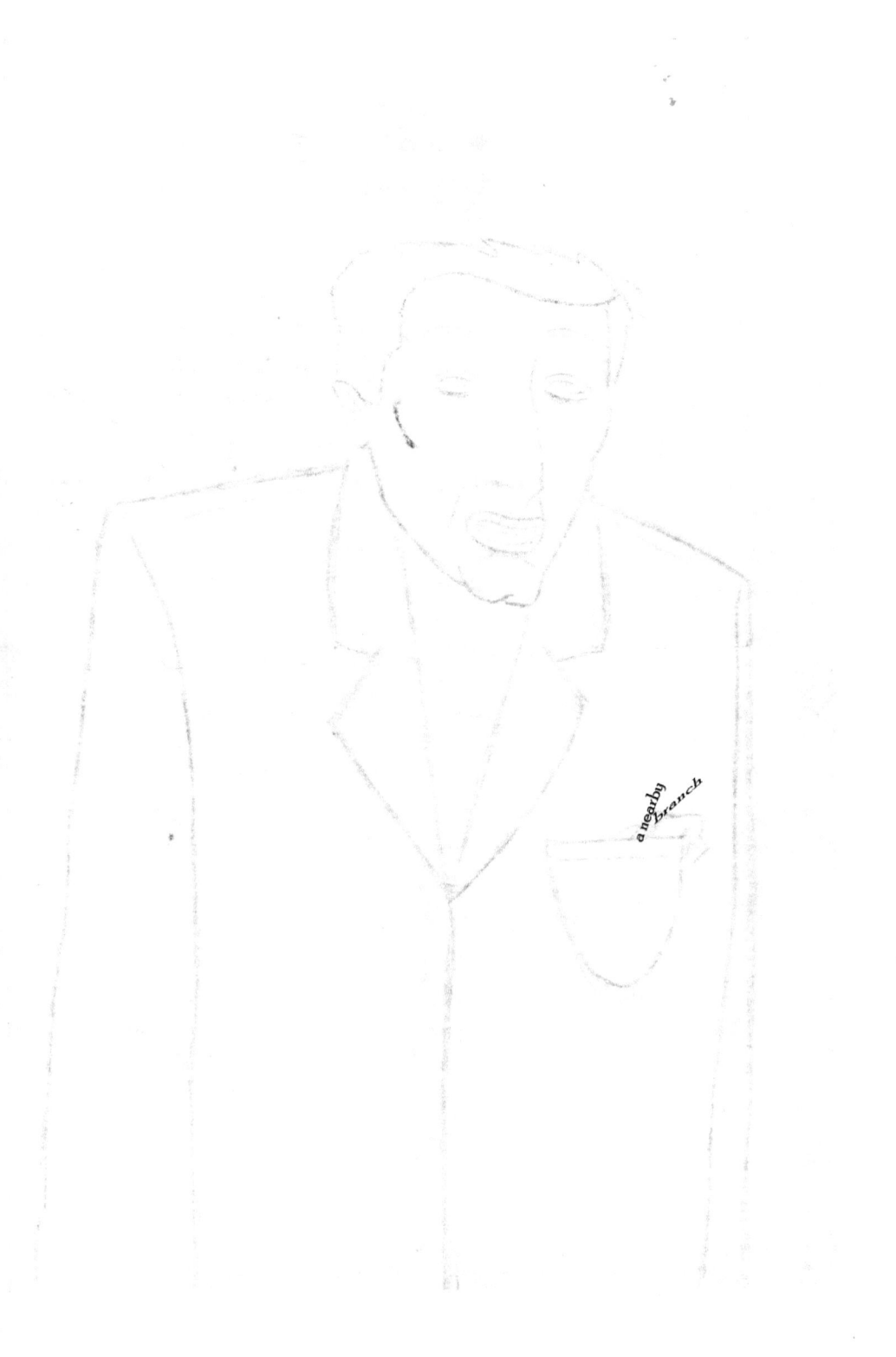

a nearby branch

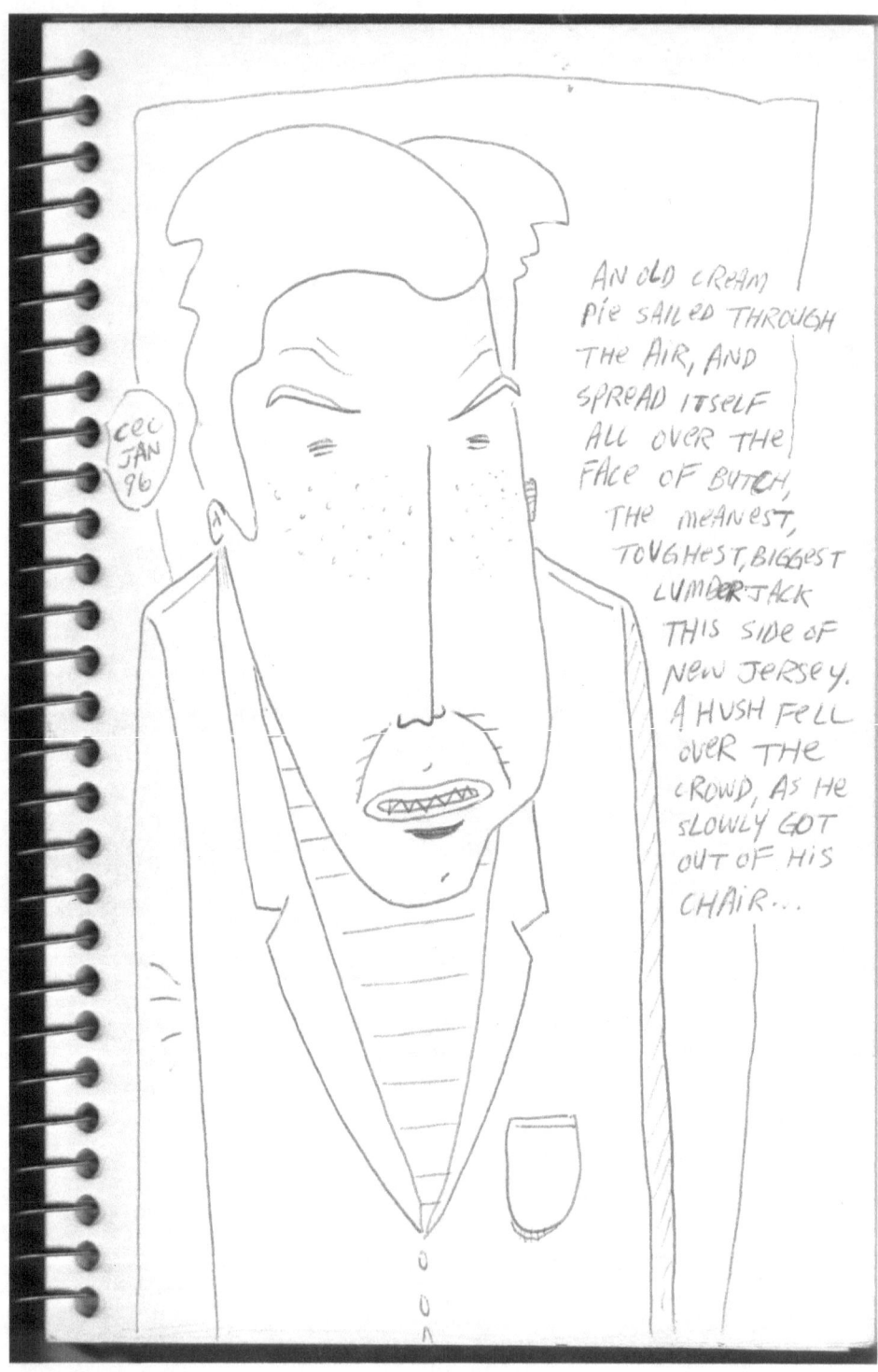

AN OLD CREAM PIE SAILED THROUGH THE AIR, AND SPREAD ITSELF ALL OVER THE FACE OF BUTCH, THE MEANEST, TOUGHEST, BIGGEST LUMBERJACK THIS SIDE OF NEW JERSEY. A HUSH FELL OVER THE CROWD, AS HE SLOWLY GOT OUT OF HIS CHAIR...

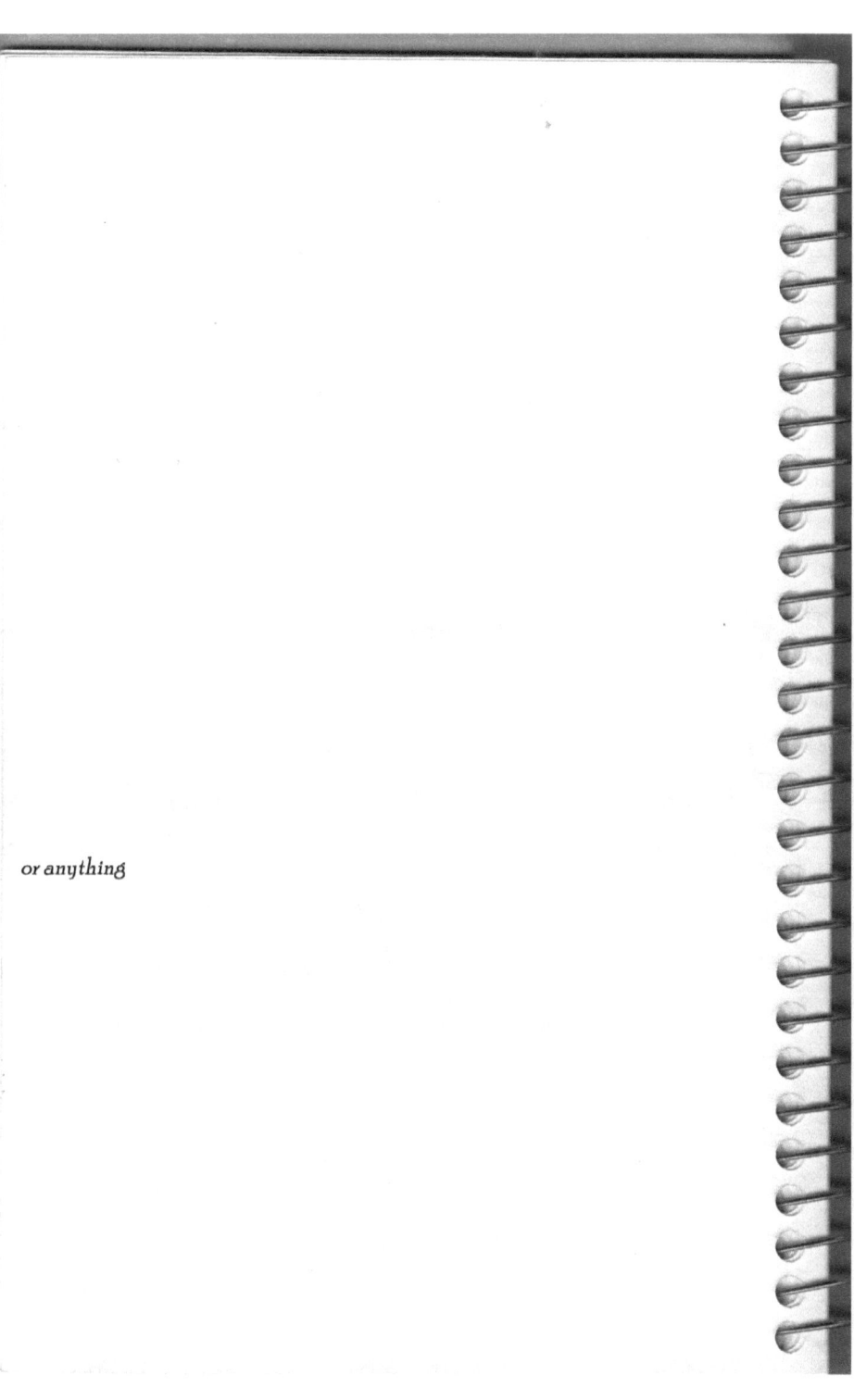

or anything

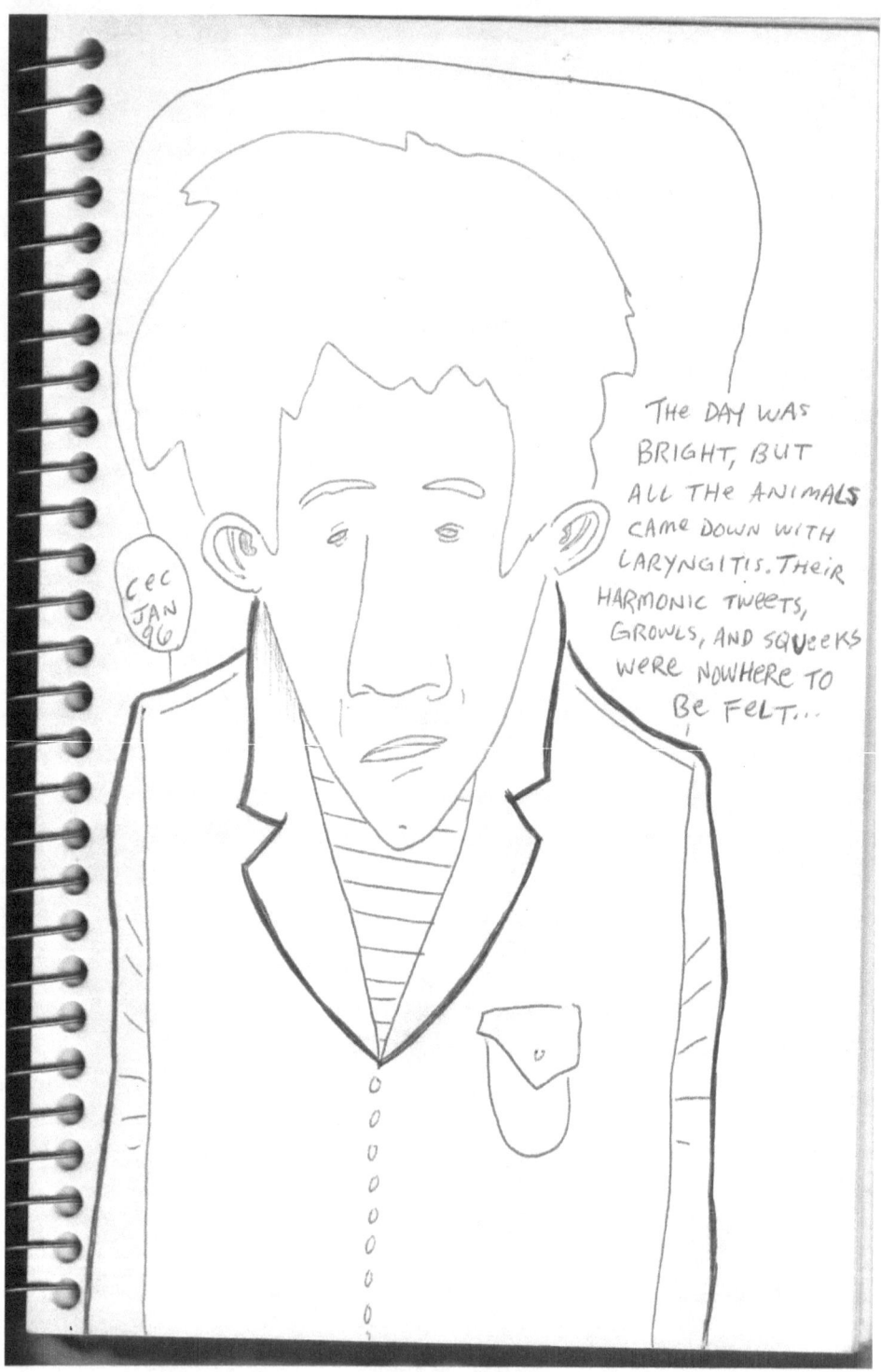

THE DAY WAS BRIGHT, BUT ALL THE ANIMALS CAME DOWN WITH LARYNGITIS. THEIR HARMONIC TWEETS, GROWLS, AND SQUEEKS WERE NOWHERE TO BE FELT...

sturdy for

SAD PICTURE

CAN'T EVEN DRAW A BOY RIDING A BICYCLE...

CRAPPY

THE SAD EXCUSE FOR AN ARTIST...

CℓC JAN 96

that matter.

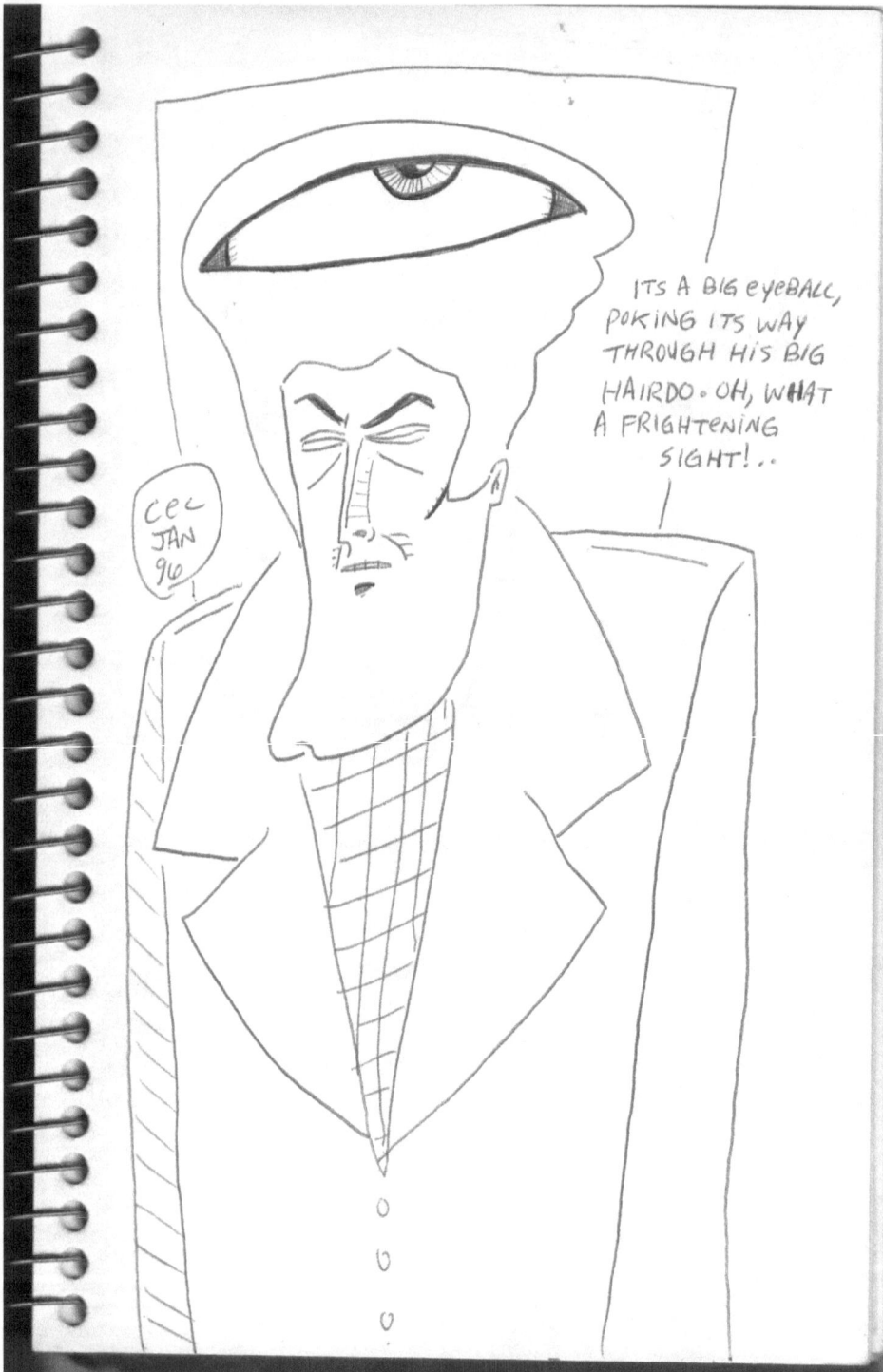

Tourists on

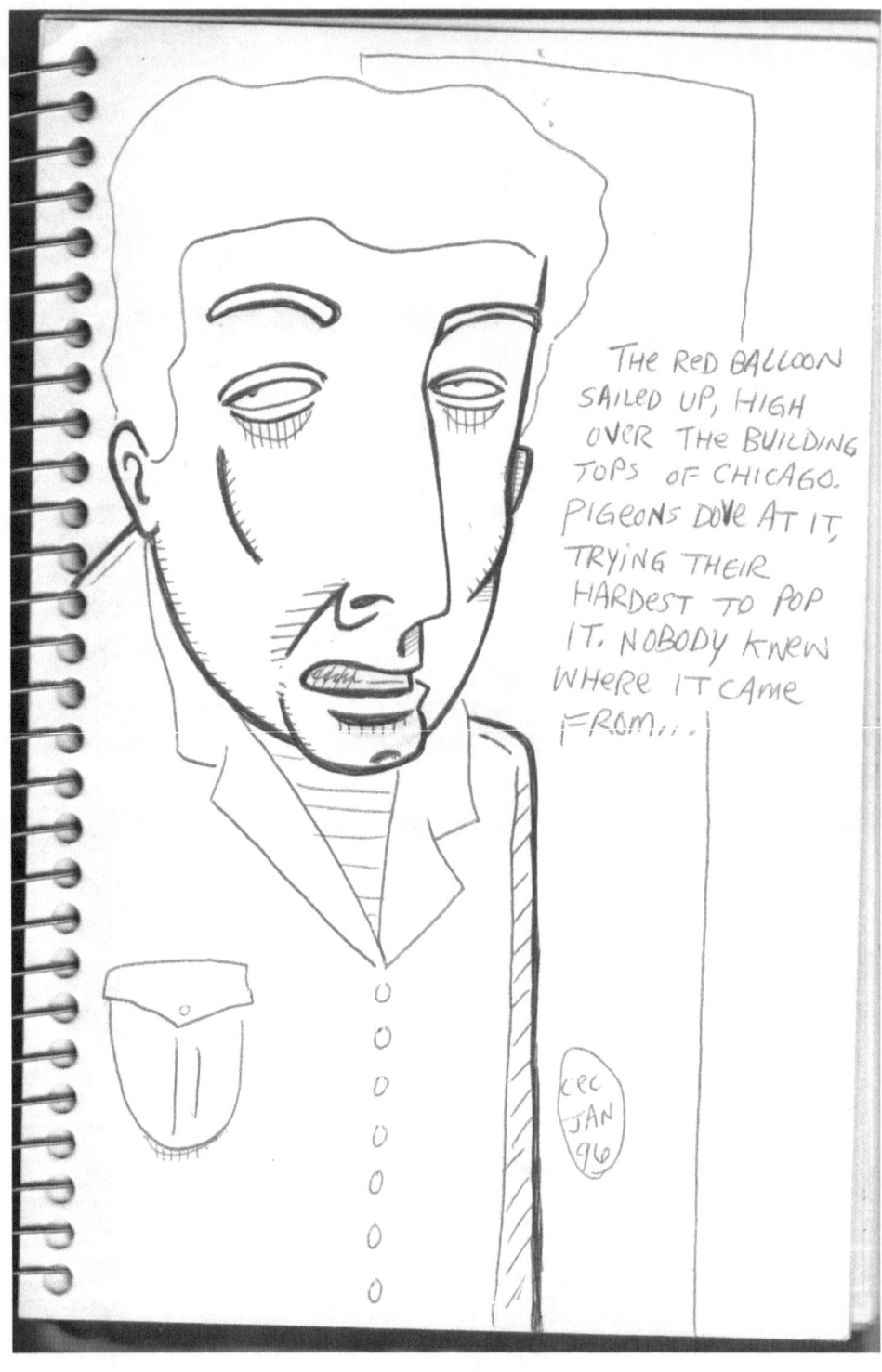

THE RED BALLOON
SAILED UP, HIGH
OVER THE BUILDING
TOPS OF CHICAGO.
PIGEONS DOVE AT IT,
TRYING THEIR
HARDEST TO POP
IT. NOBODY KNEW
WHERE IT CAME
FROM...

CPC
JAN
96

a bridge

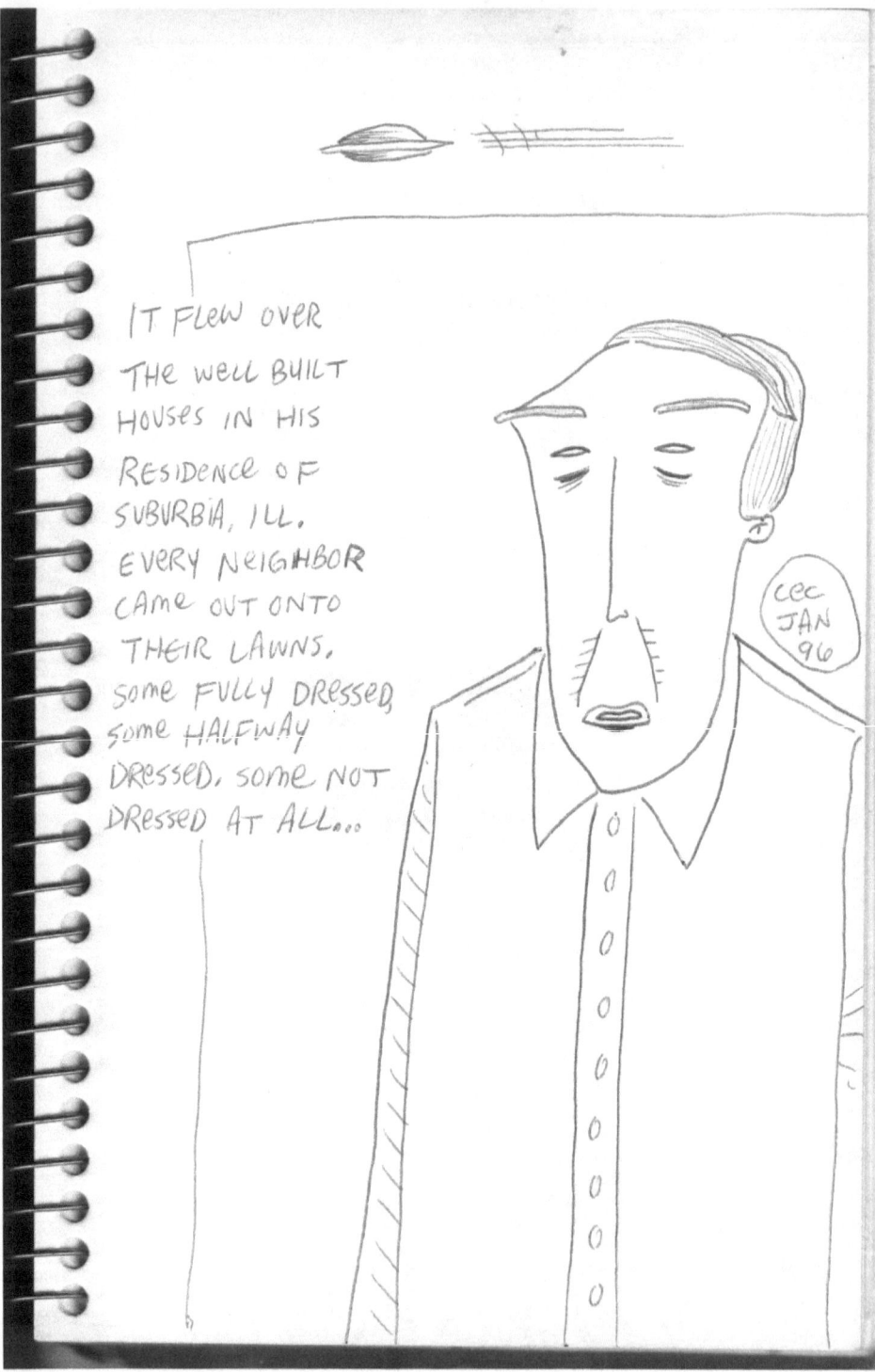

overhead are

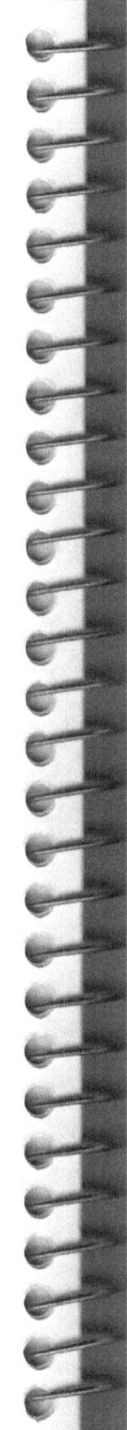

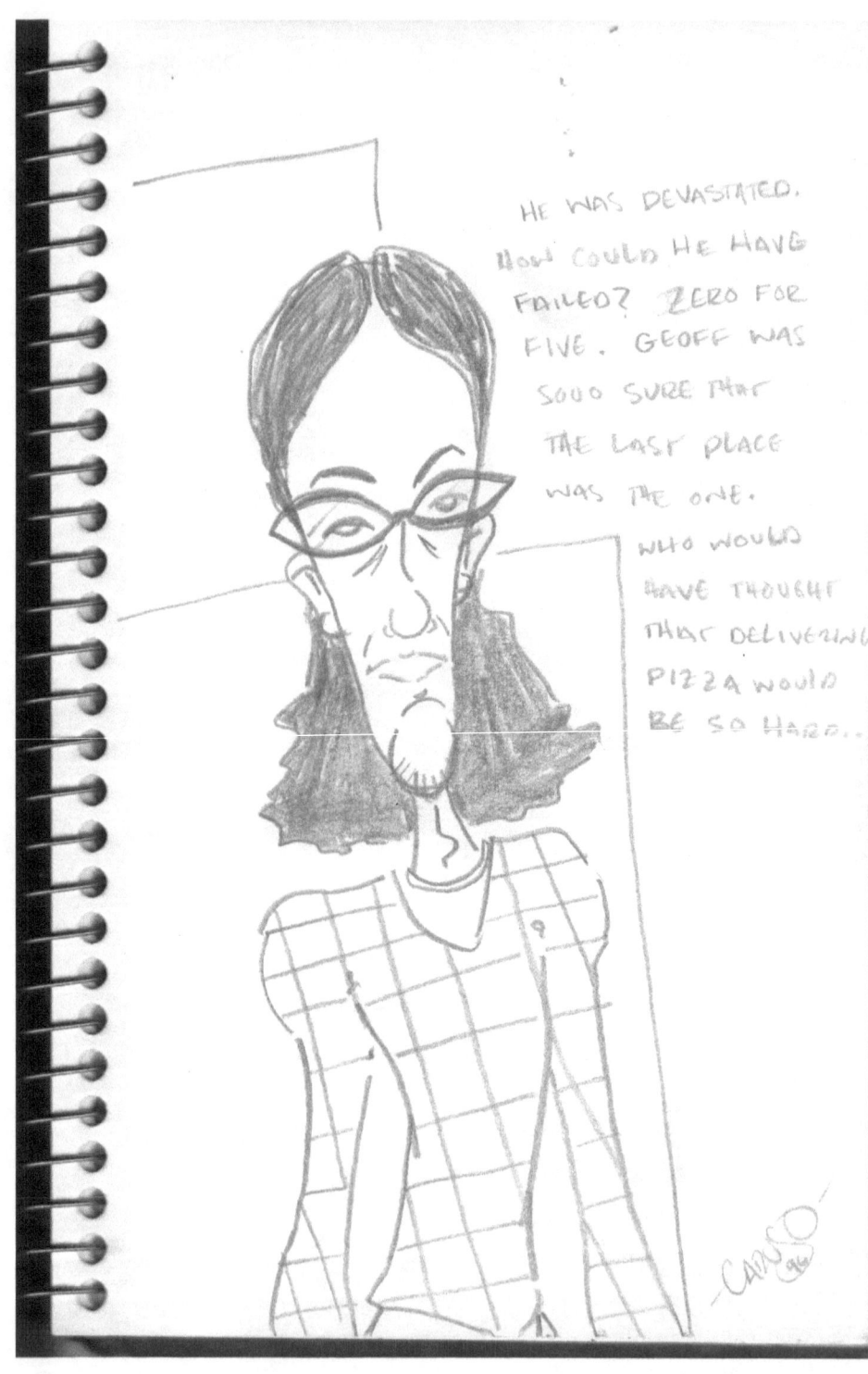

taking pictures of

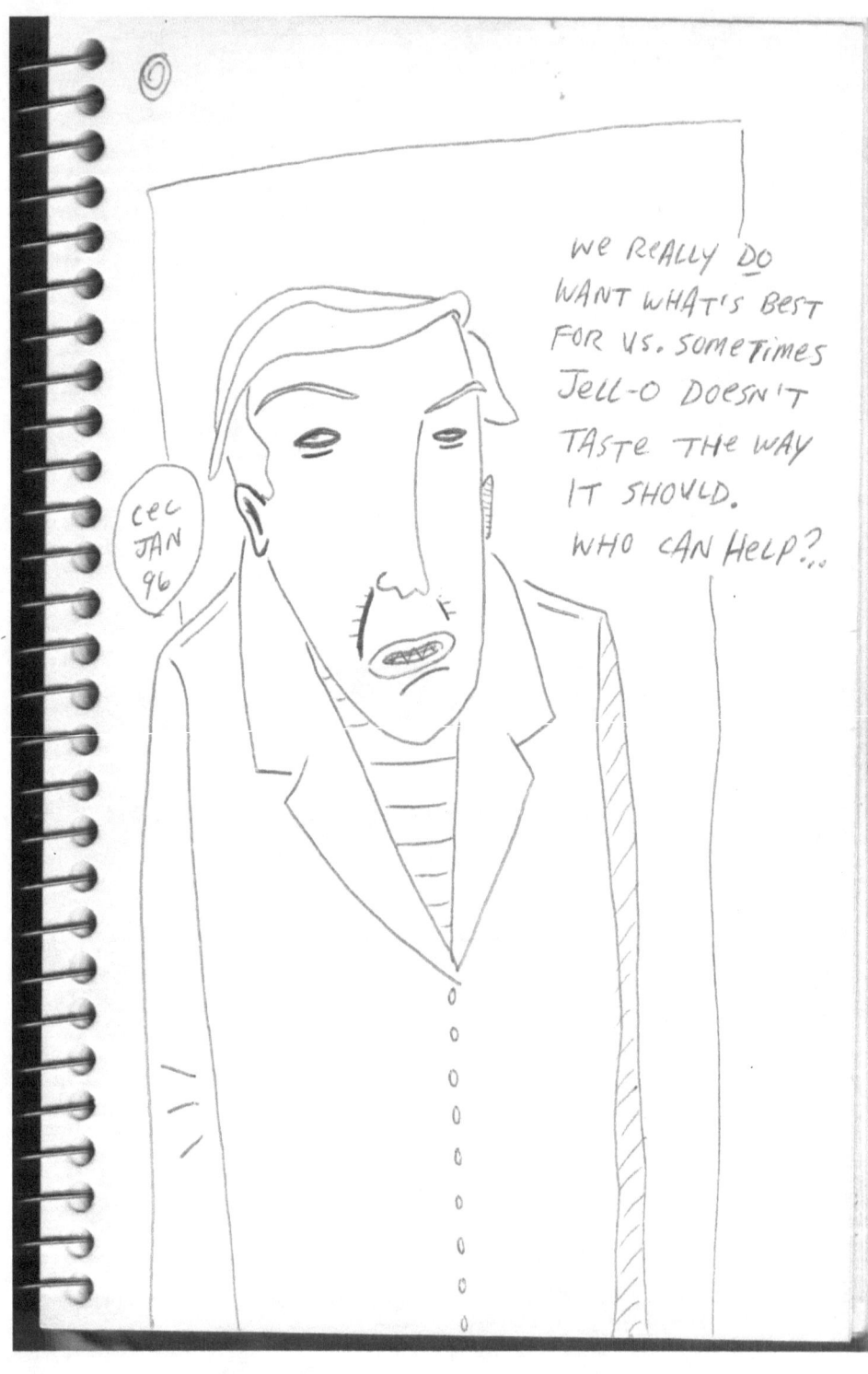

what they

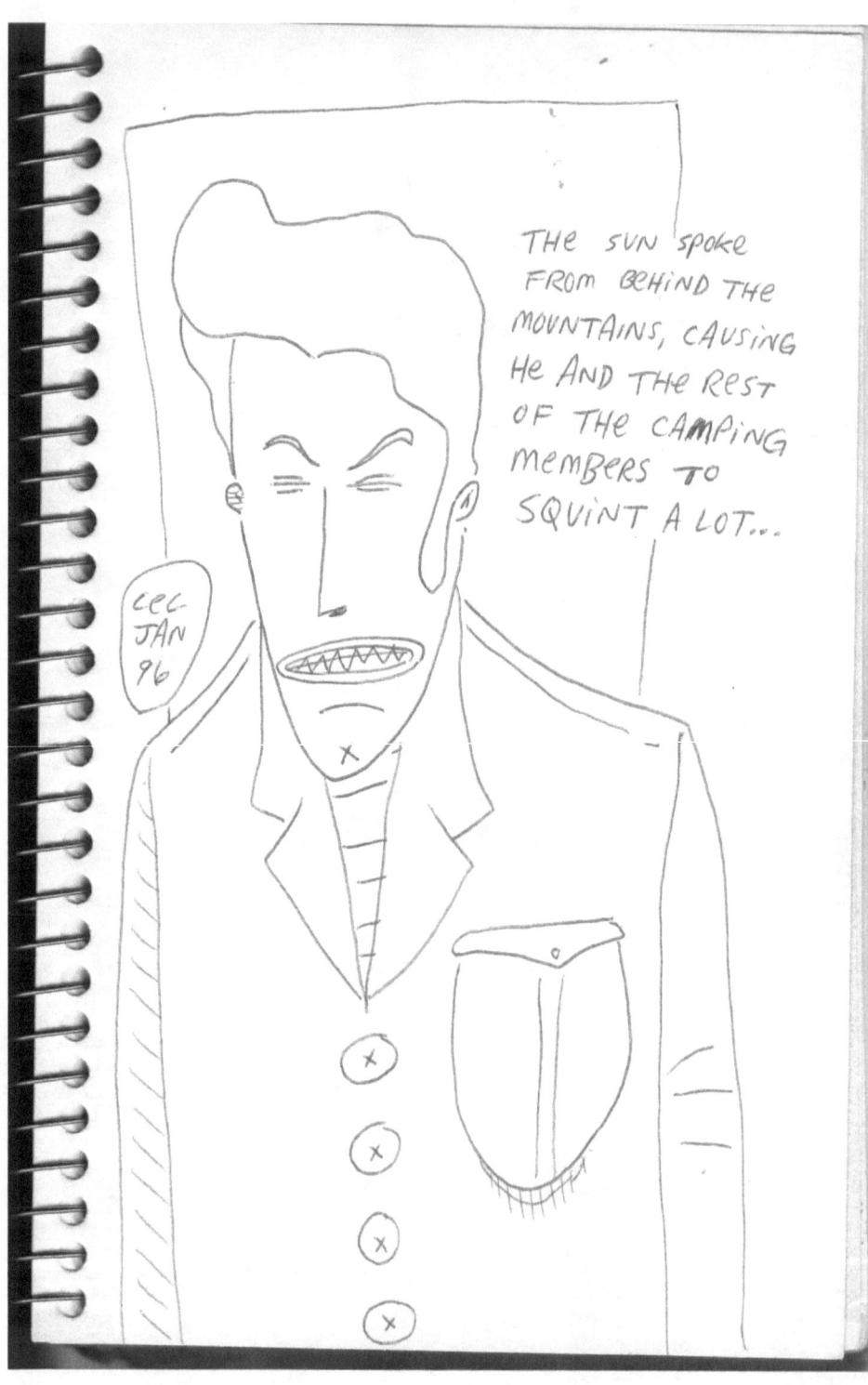

believe is

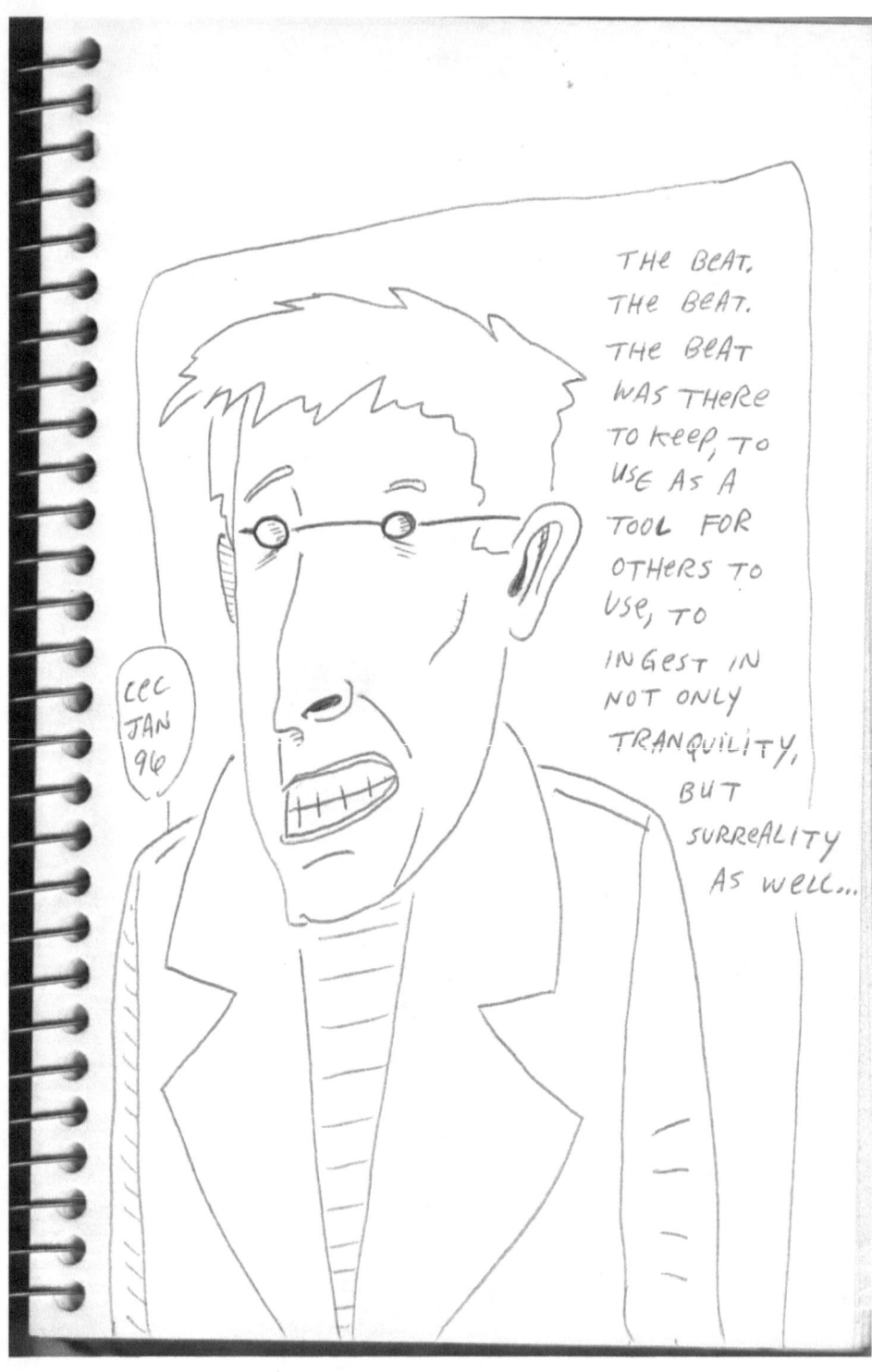

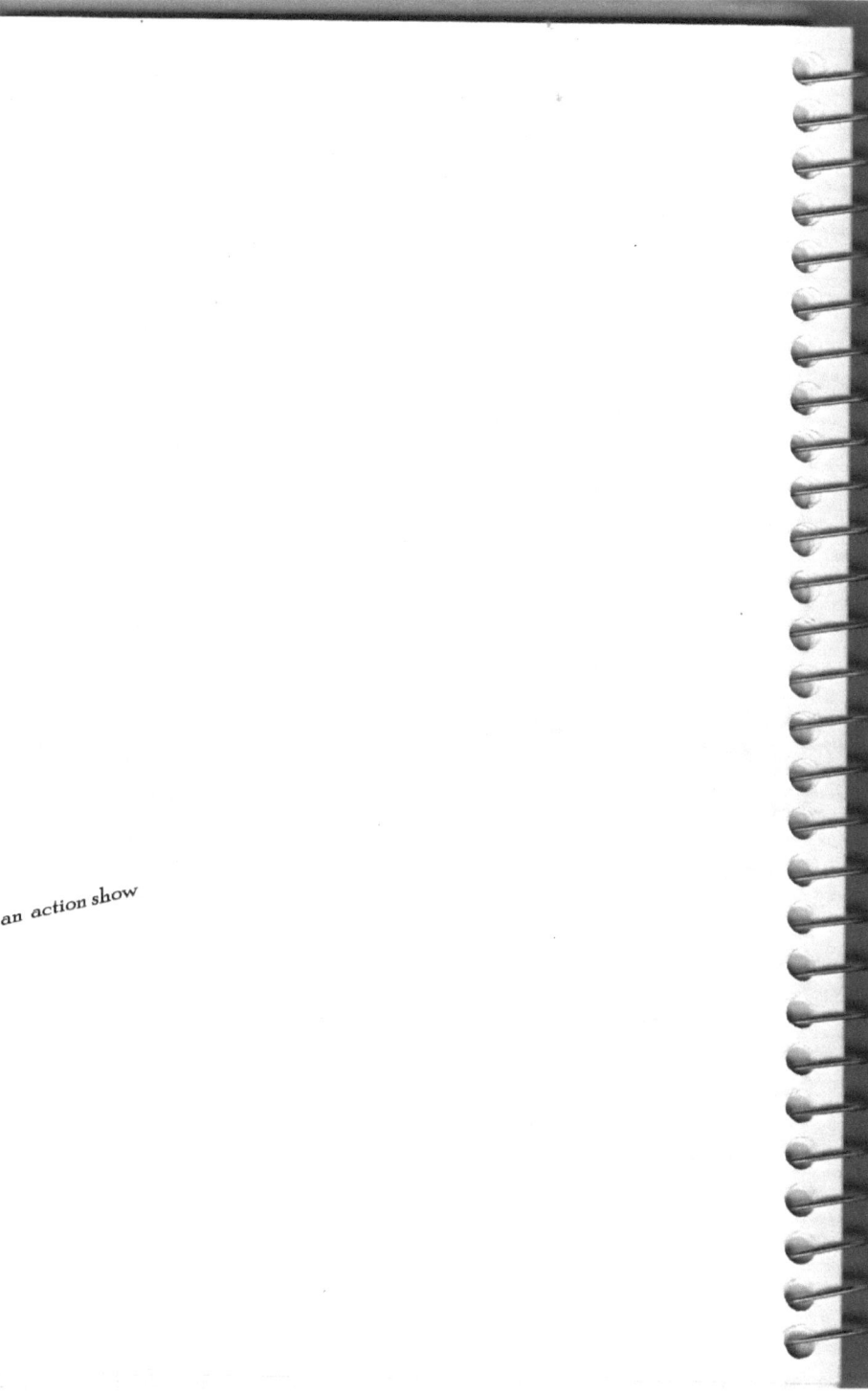

an action show

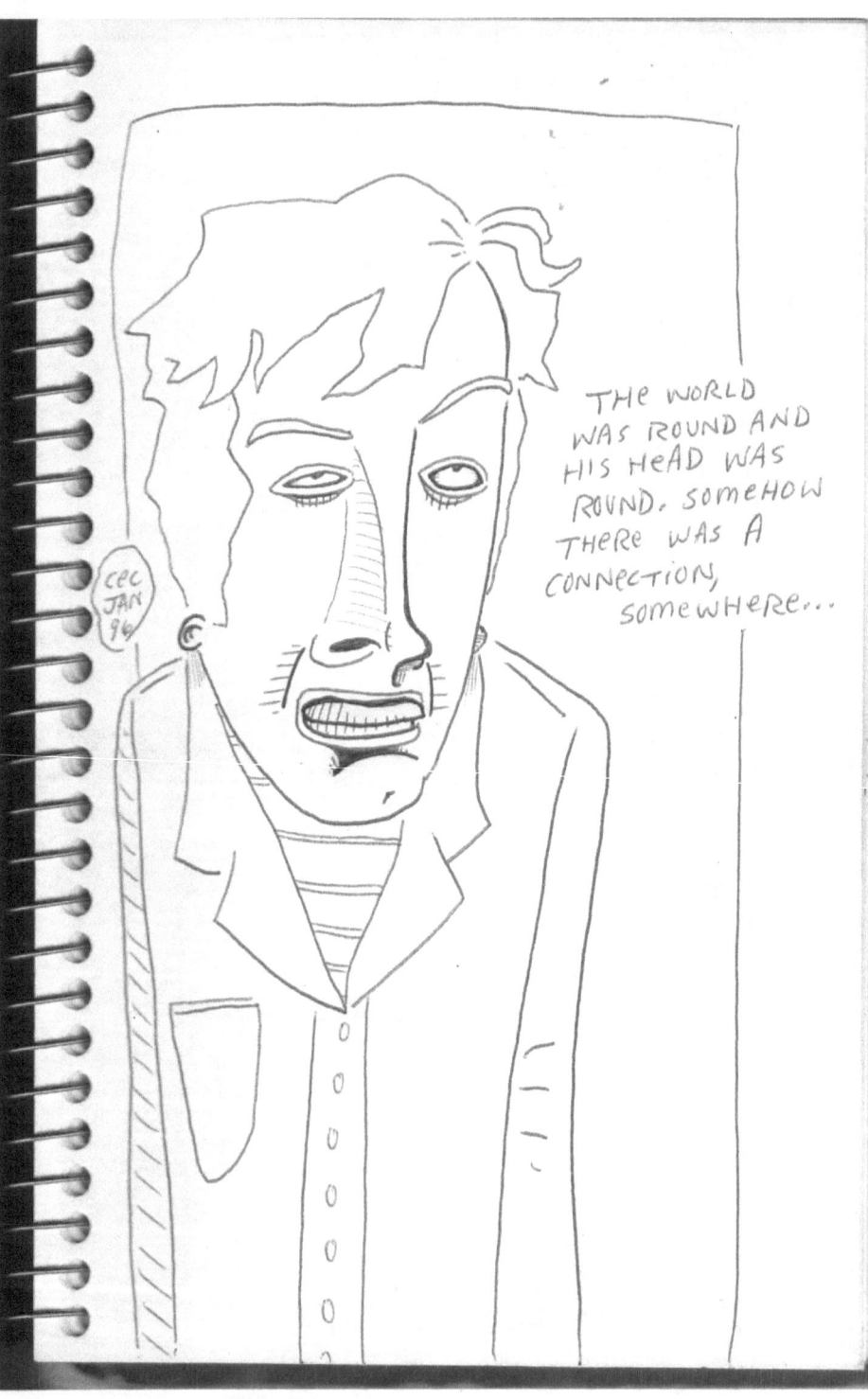

put on by

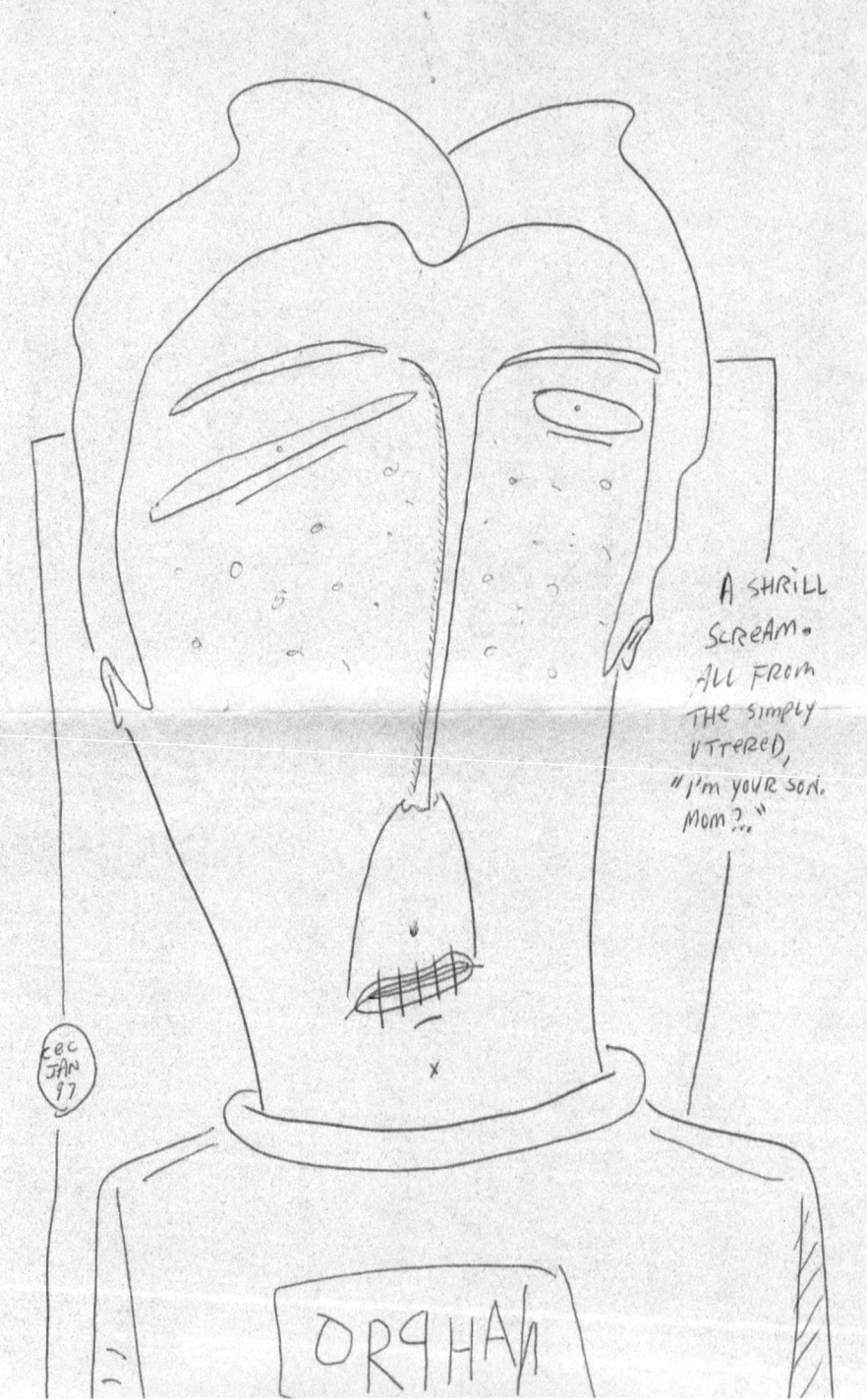

a professional

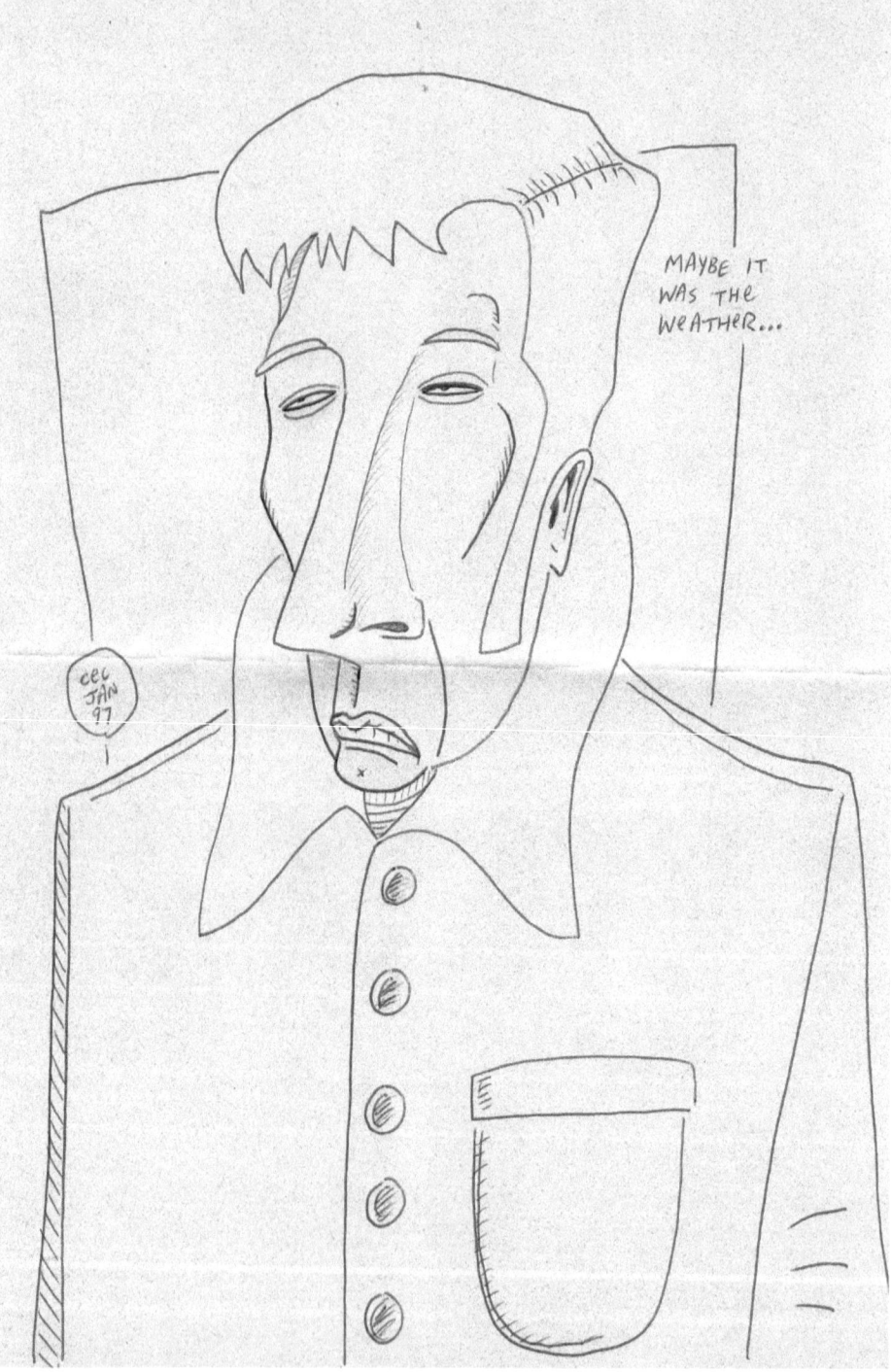

stuntman employed

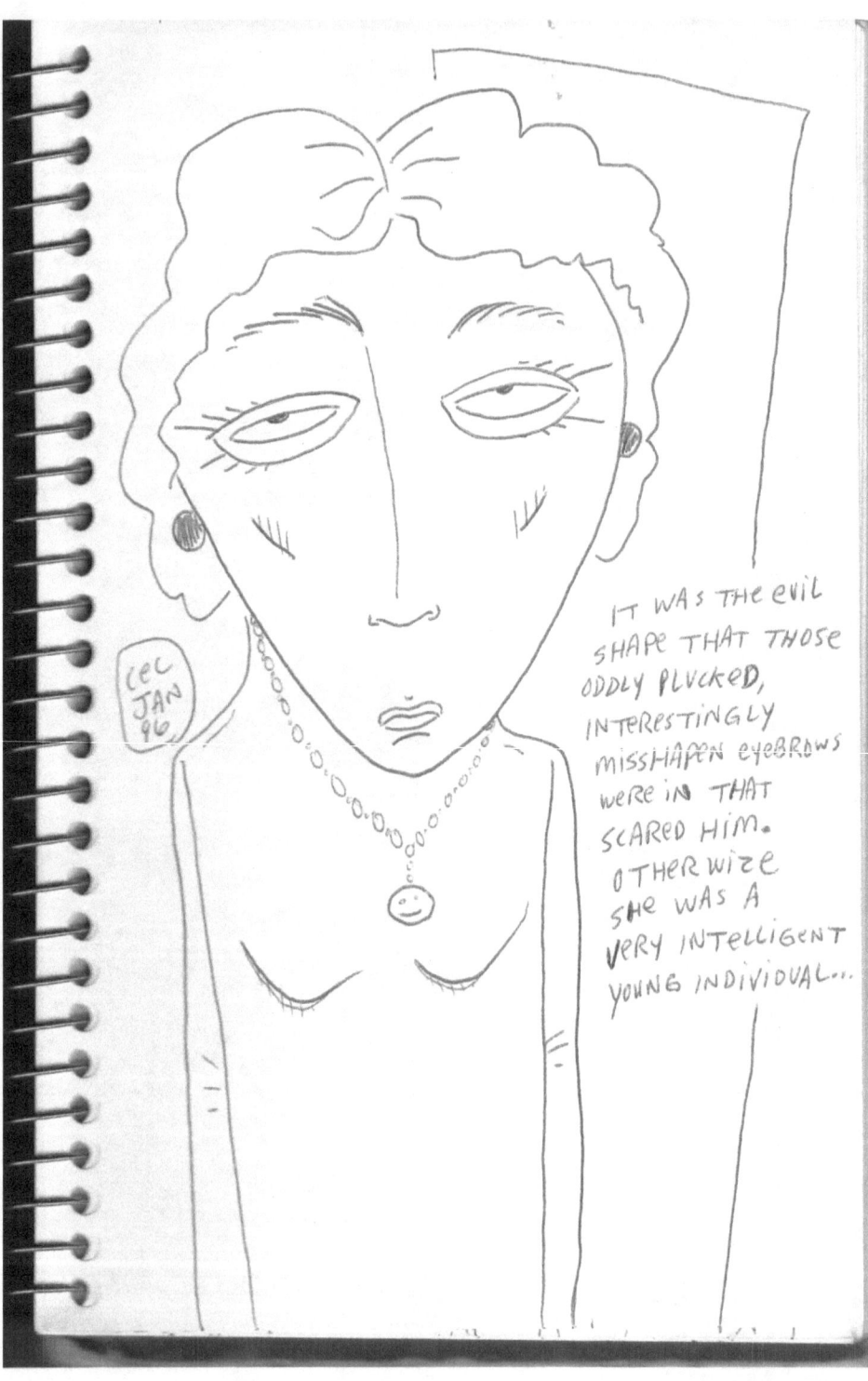

IT WAS THE EVIL
SHAPE THAT THOSE
ODDLY PLUCKED,
INTERESTINGLY
MISSHAPEN EYEBROWS
WERE IN THAT
SCARED HIM.
OTHERWIZE
SHE WAS A
VERY INTELLIGENT
YOUNG INDIVIDUAL...

by the

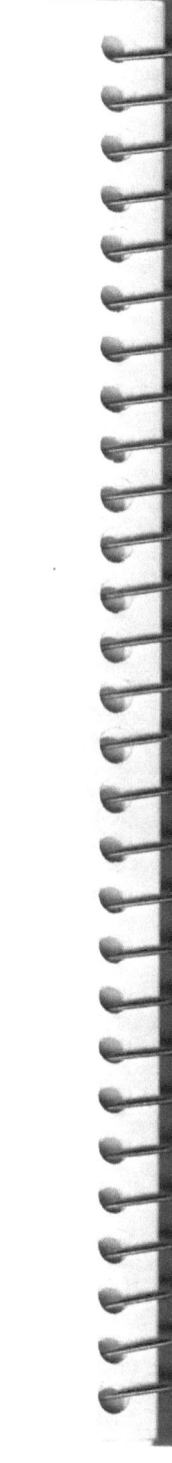

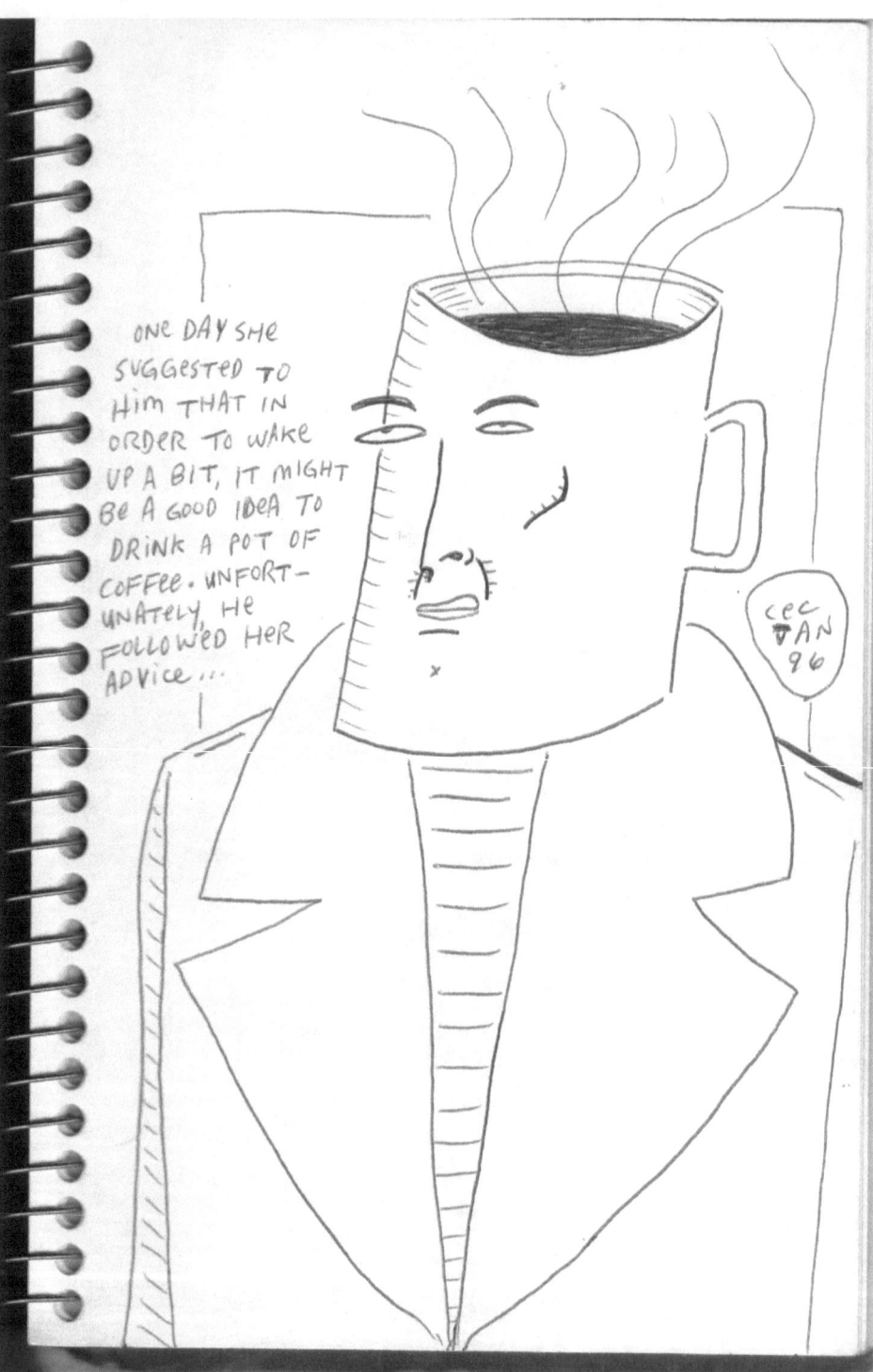

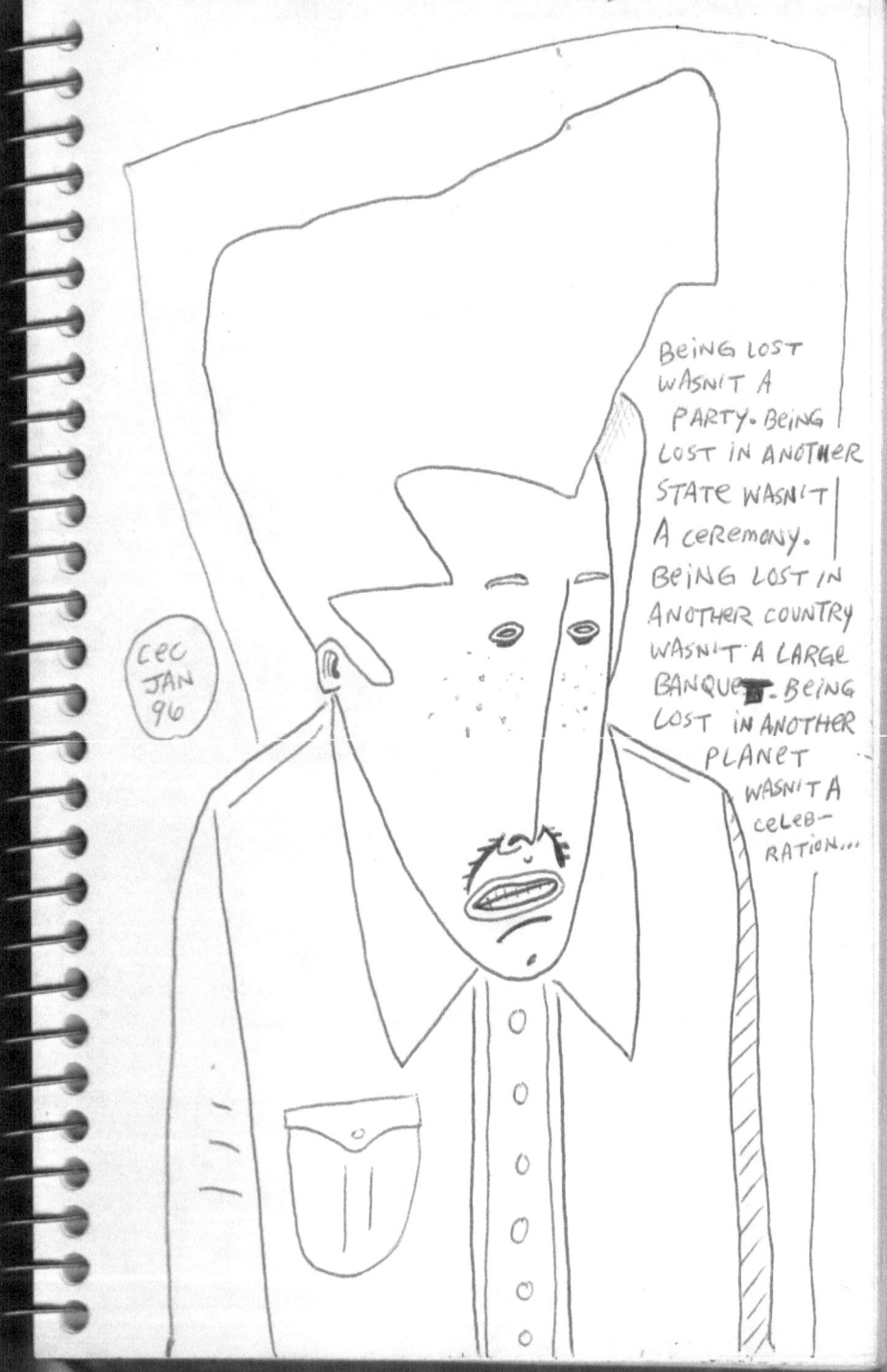

hired by the

He escaped from the evil clutches of Mr. Swanson, P.T. Barnum's demented cousin...

cec JAN 96

traveling agency

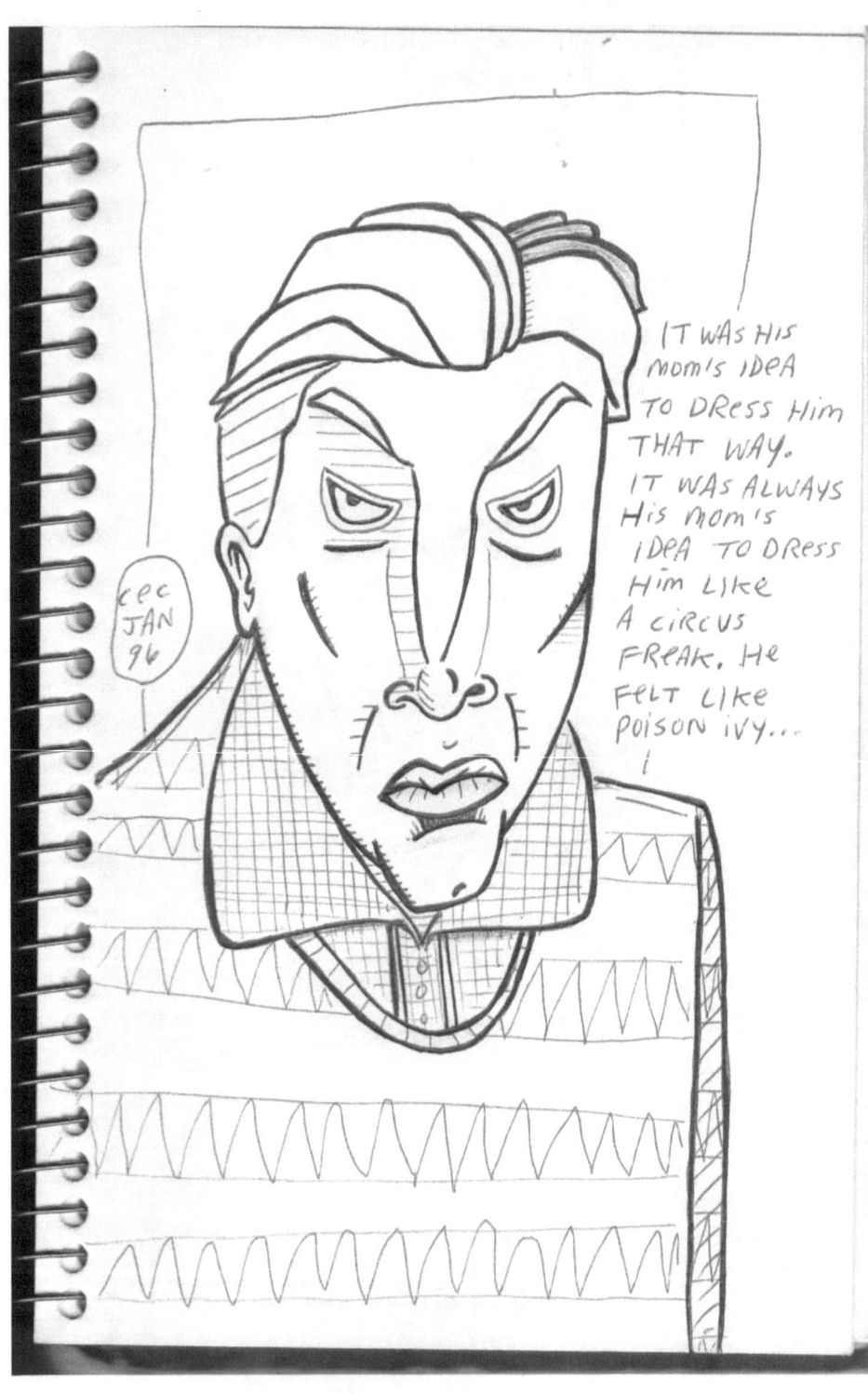

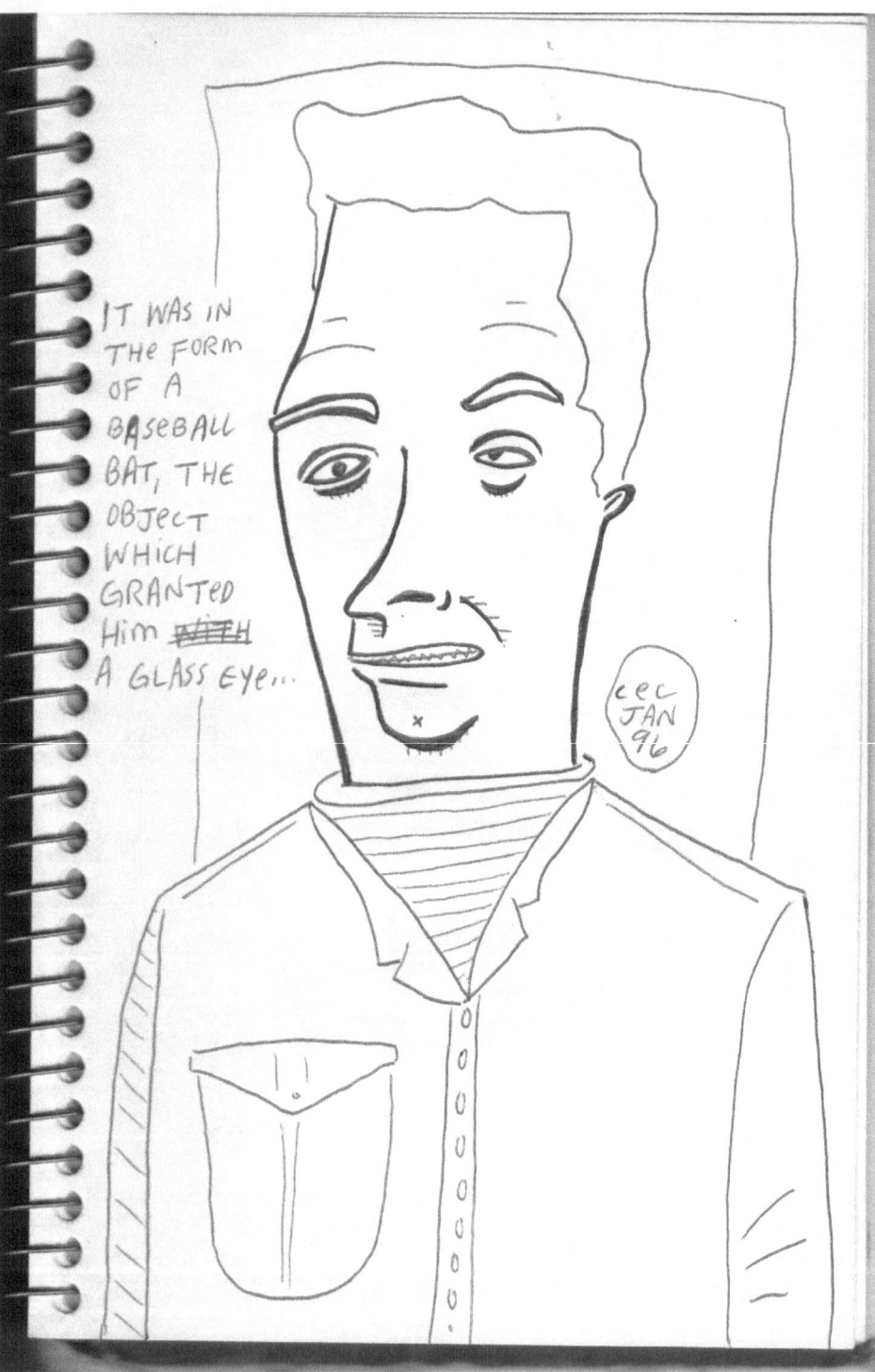

them around

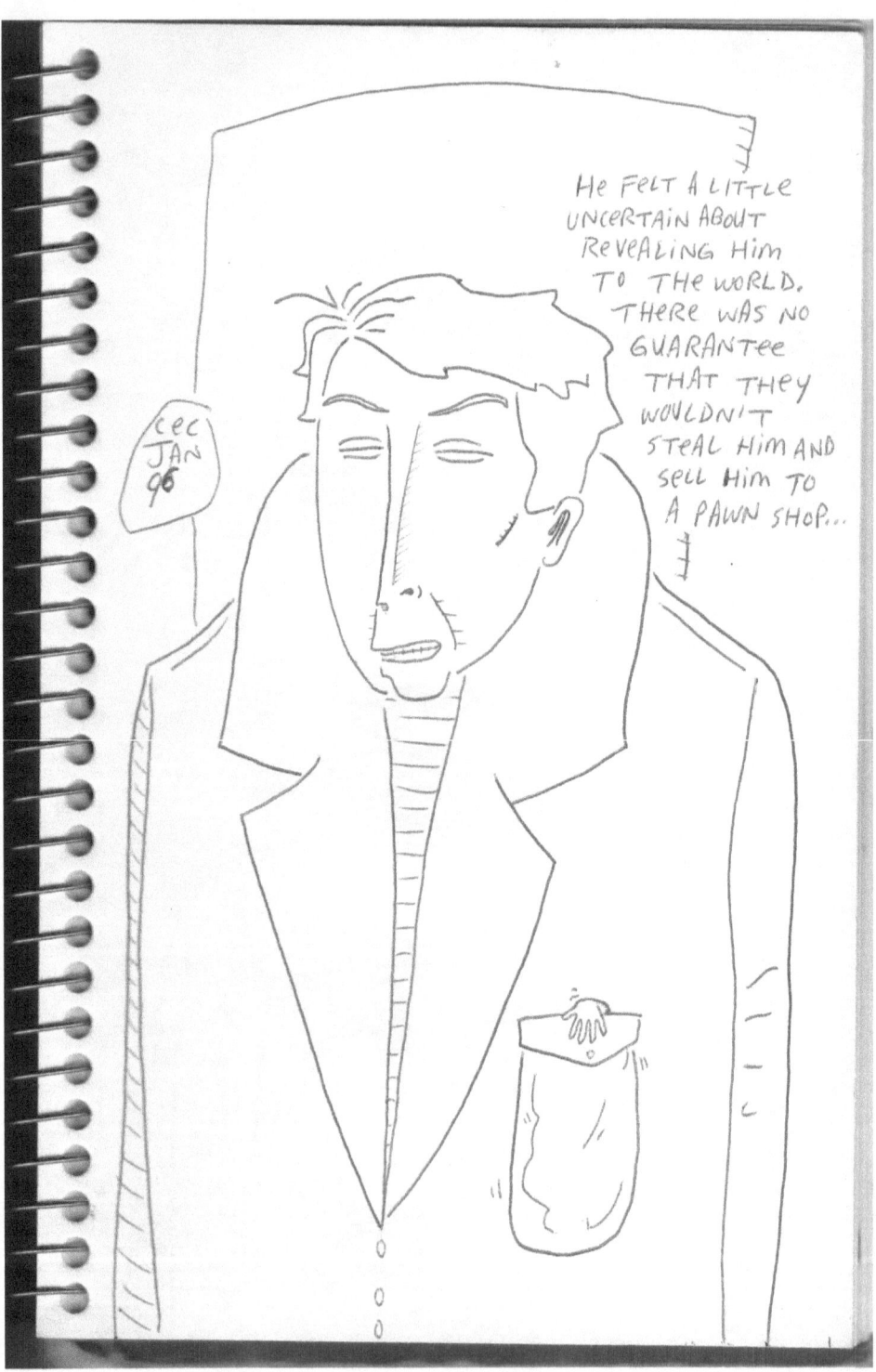

through the

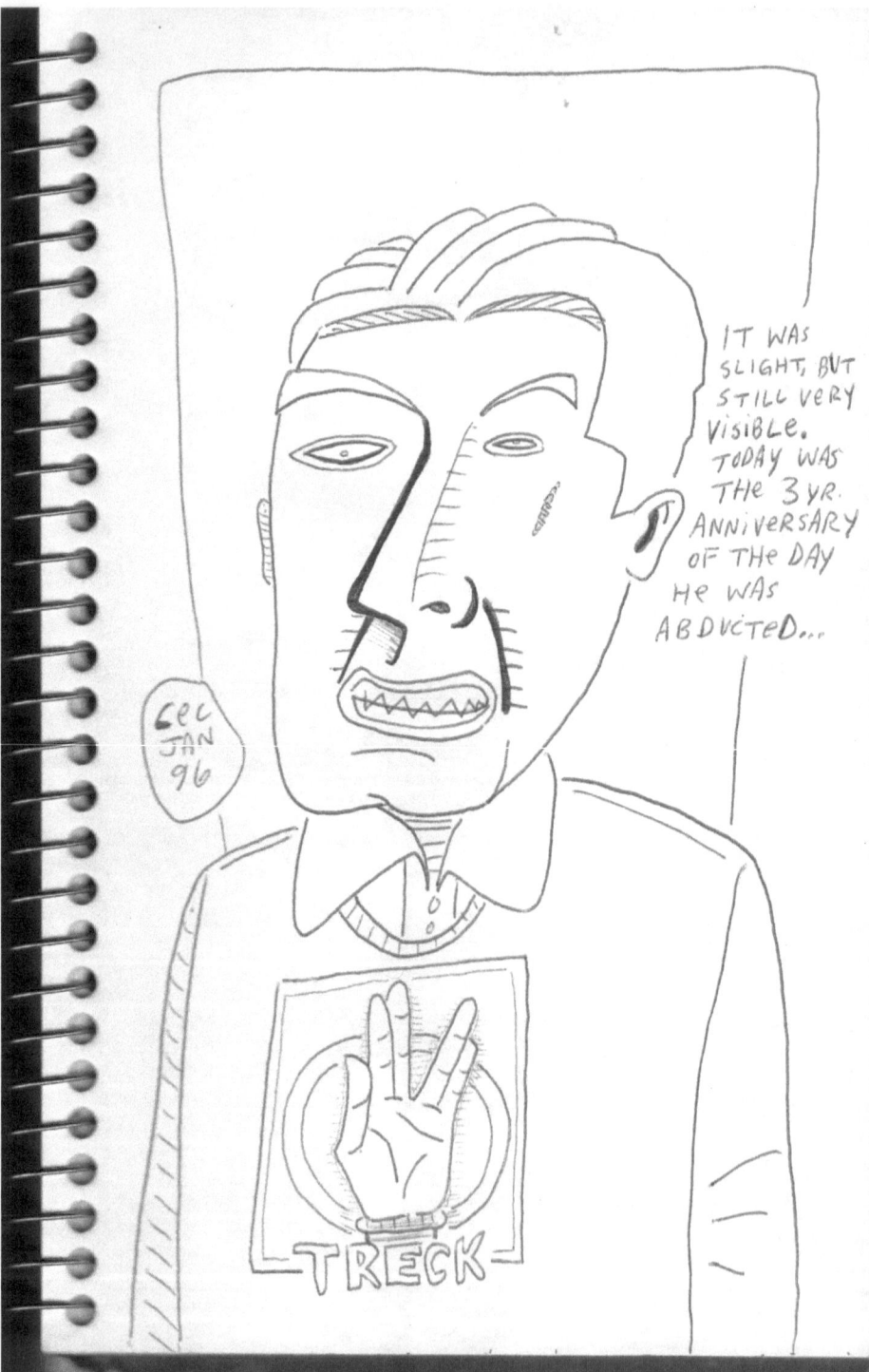

land. They

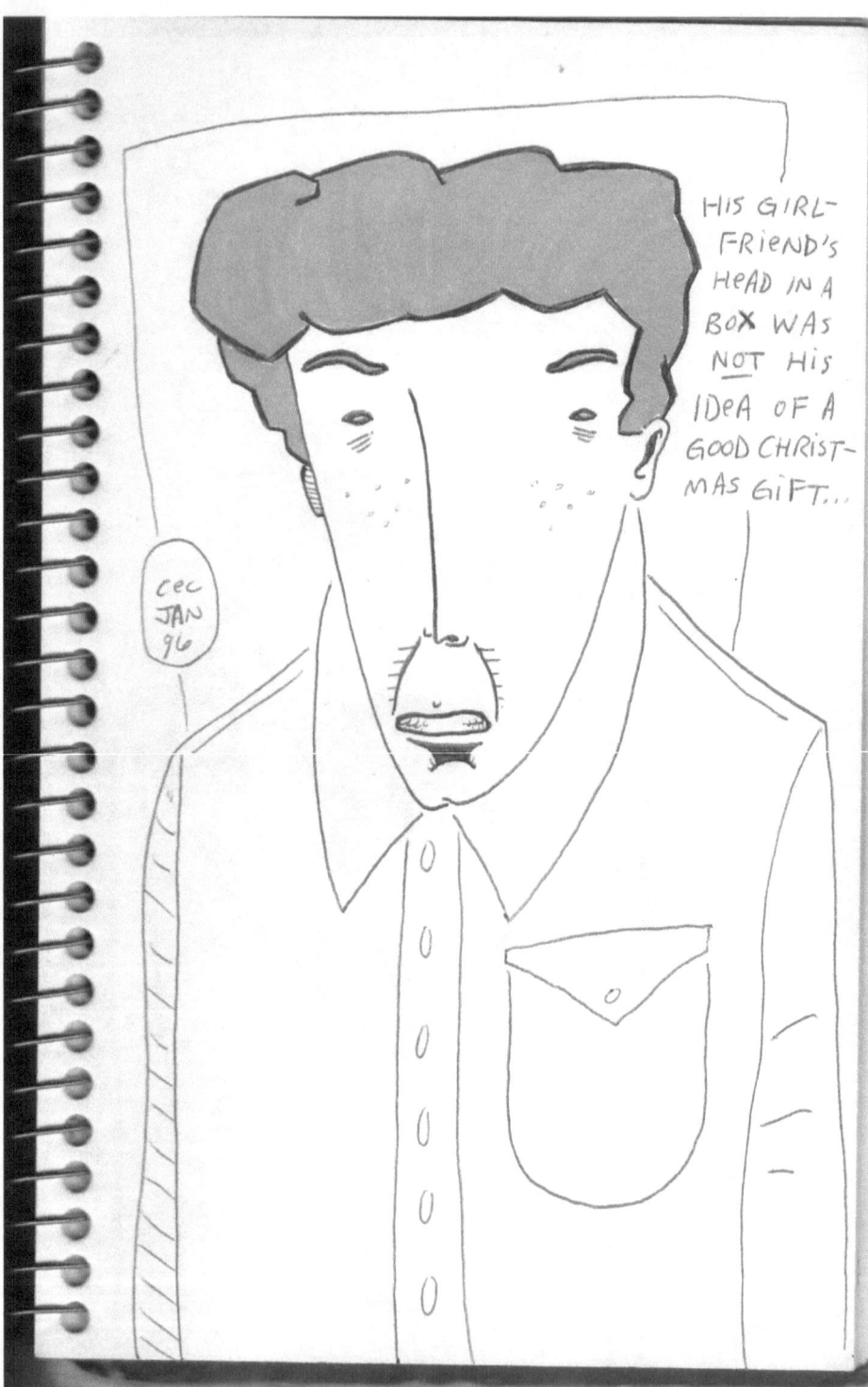

are delighted!

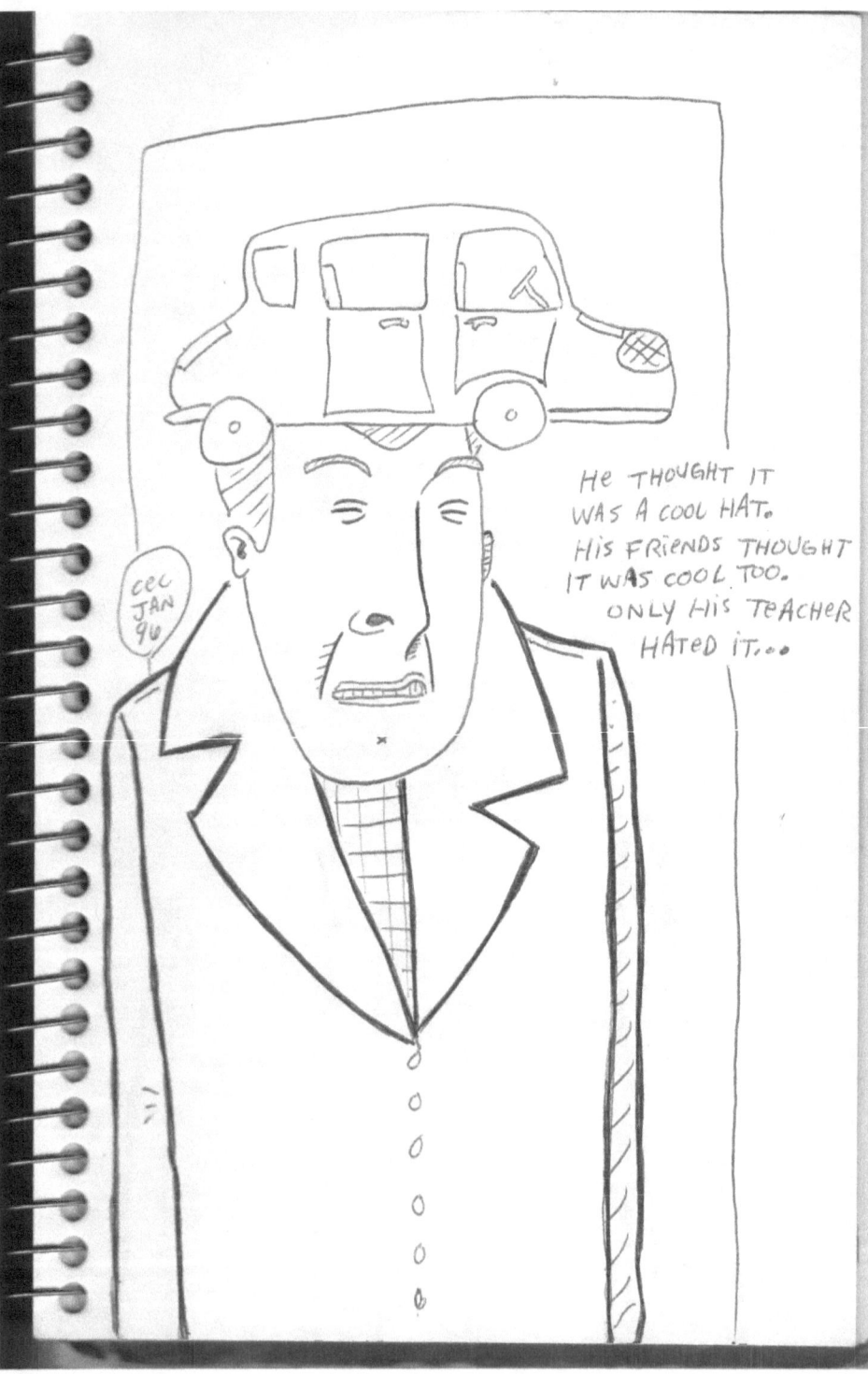

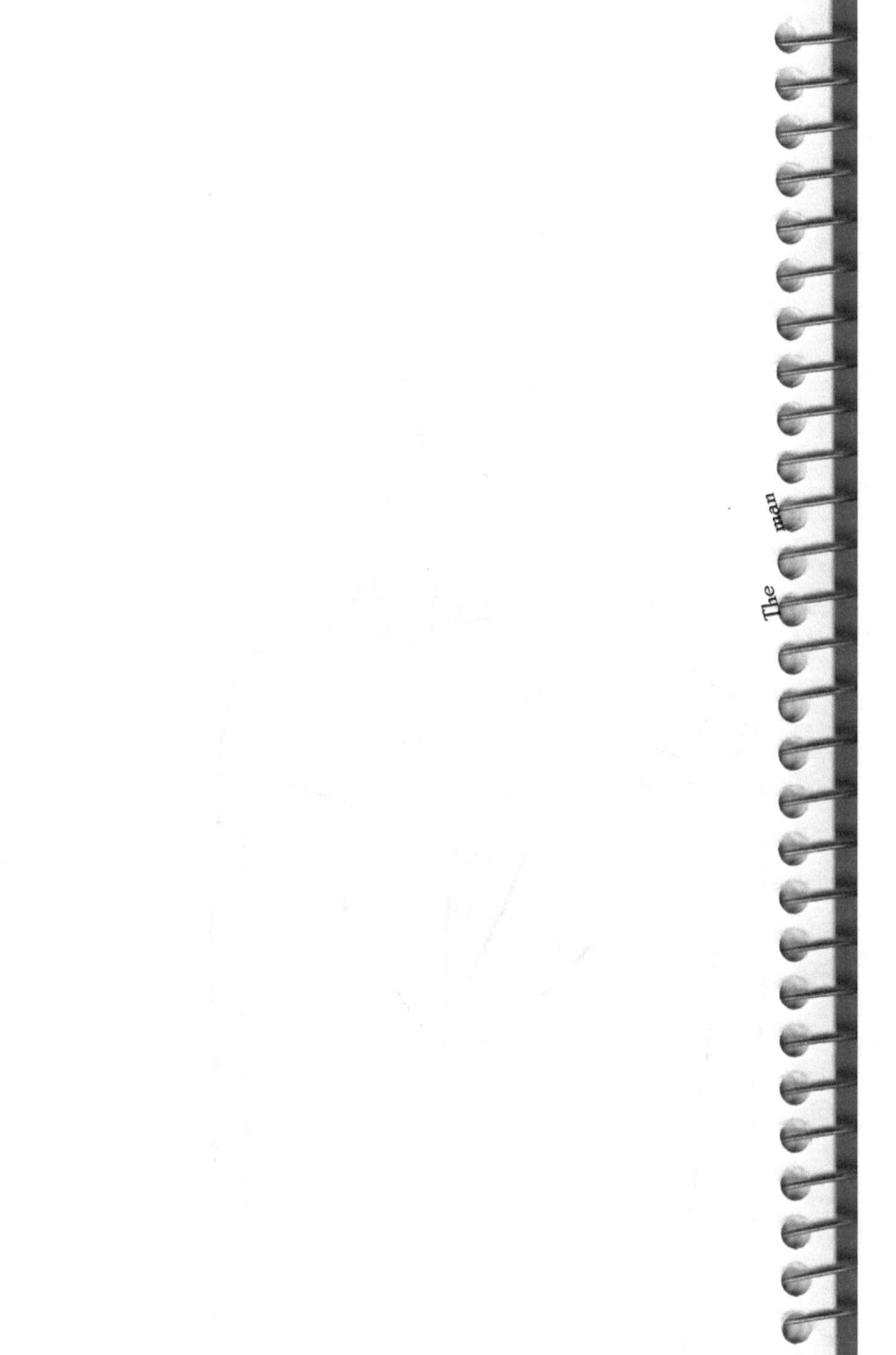

The man

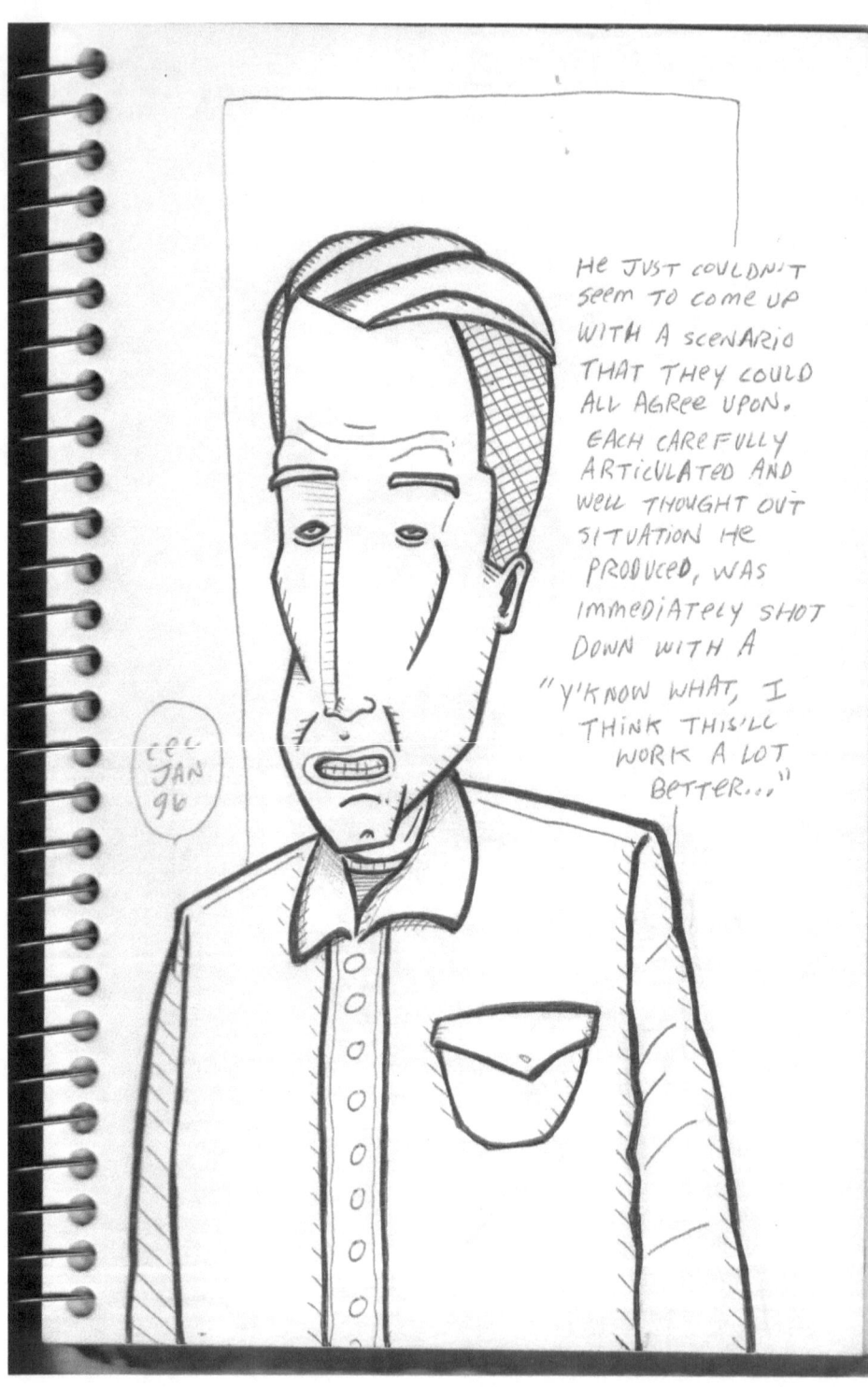

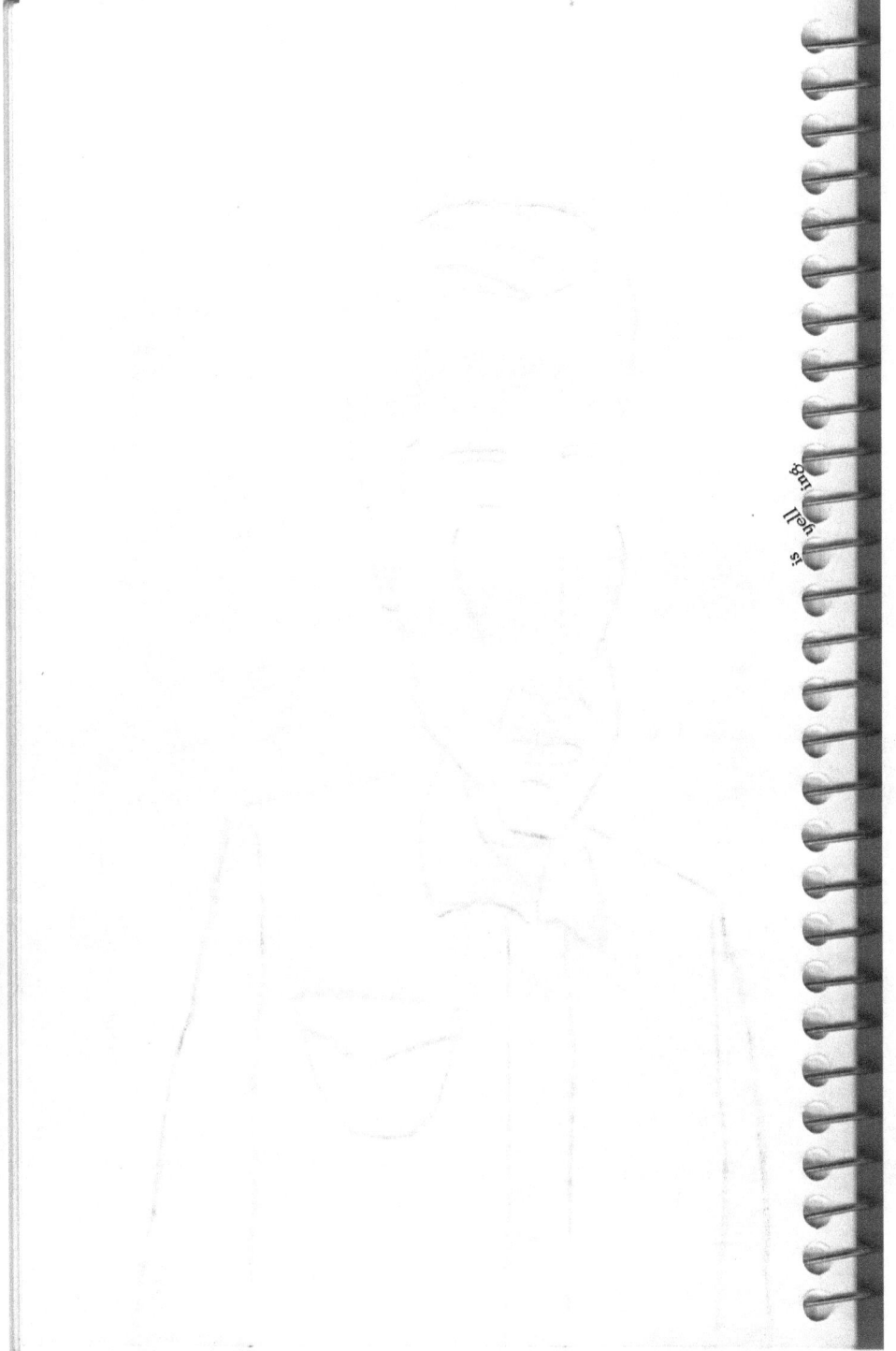

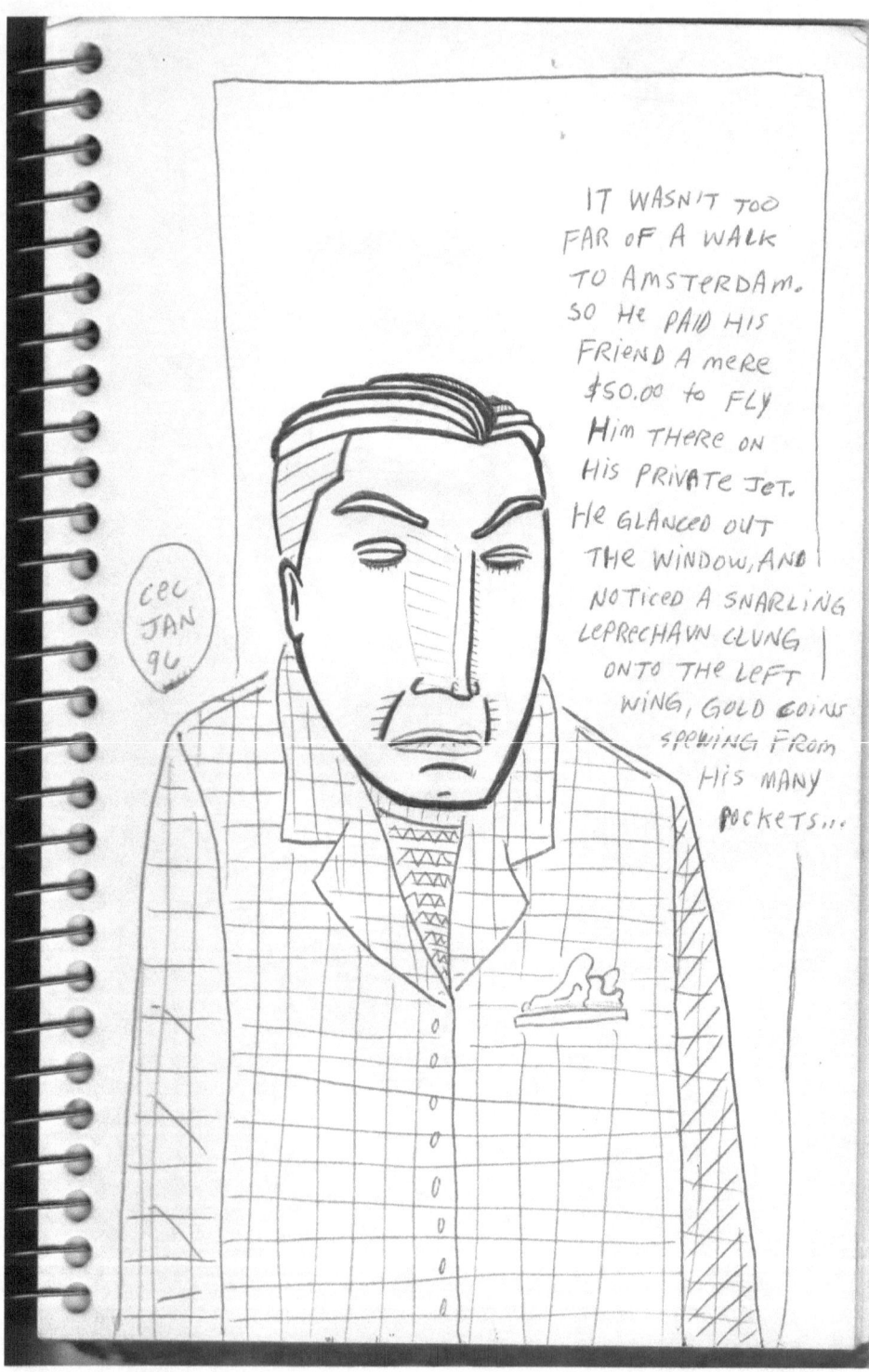

They are

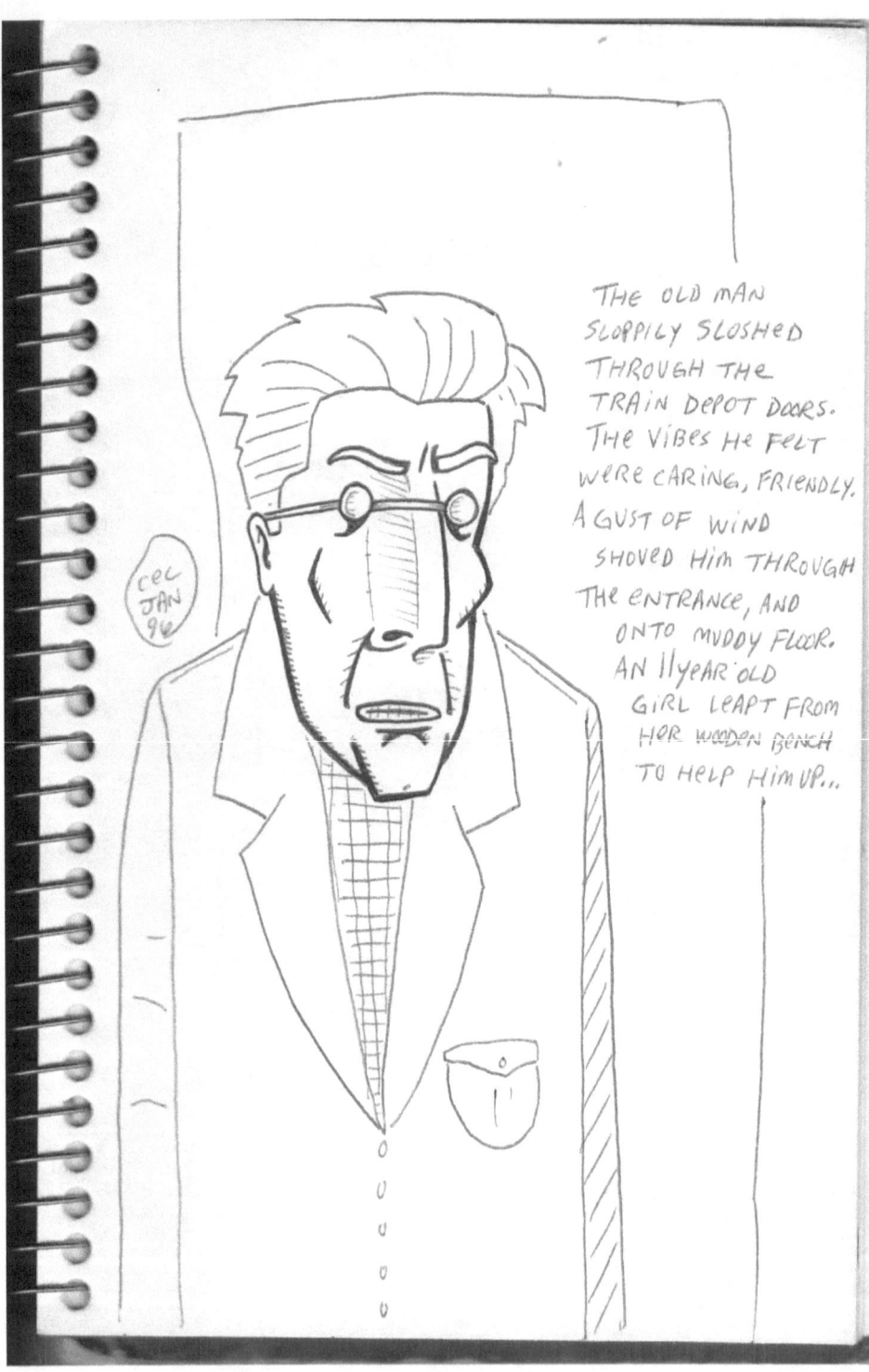

THE OLD MAN SLOPPILY SLOSHED THROUGH THE TRAIN DEPOT DOORS. THE VIBES HE FELT WERE CARING, FRIENDLY. A GUST OF WIND SHOVED HIM THROUGH THE ENTRANCE, AND ONTO MUDDY FLOOR. AN 11 YEAR OLD GIRL LEAPT FROM HER WOODEN BENCH TO HELP HIM UP...

yelling and

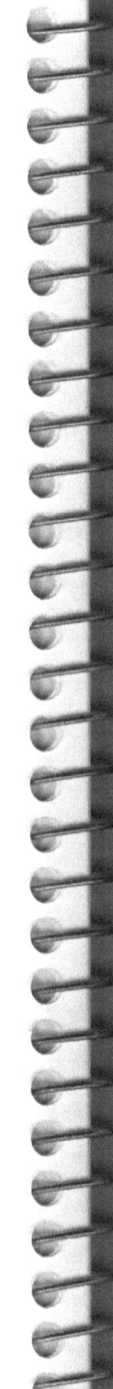

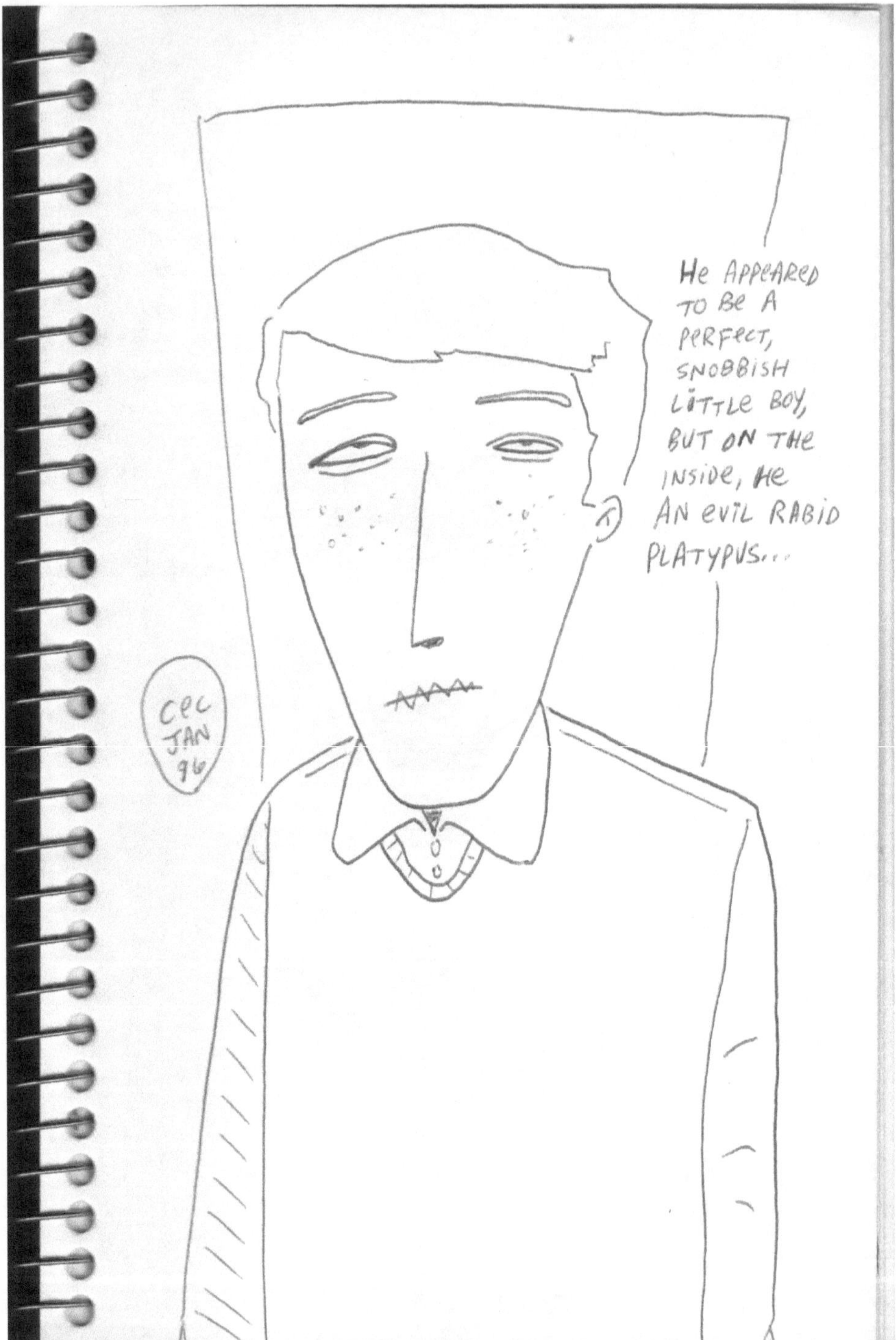
He APPEARED TO BE A PERFECT, SNOBBISH LITTLE BOY, BUT ON THE INSIDE, HE AN EVIL RABID PLATYPUS...
CEC JAN 96

waving. They

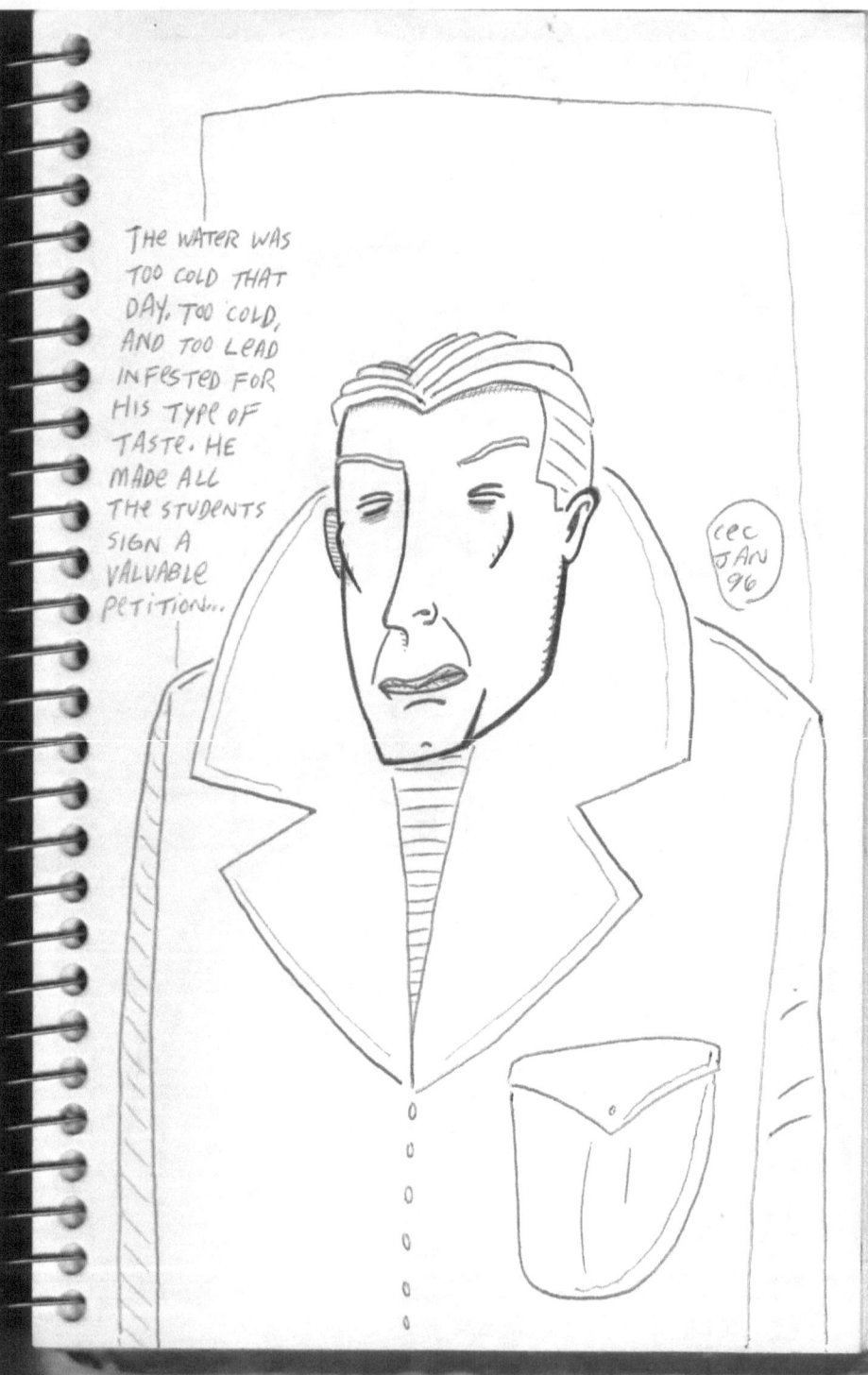

continue this

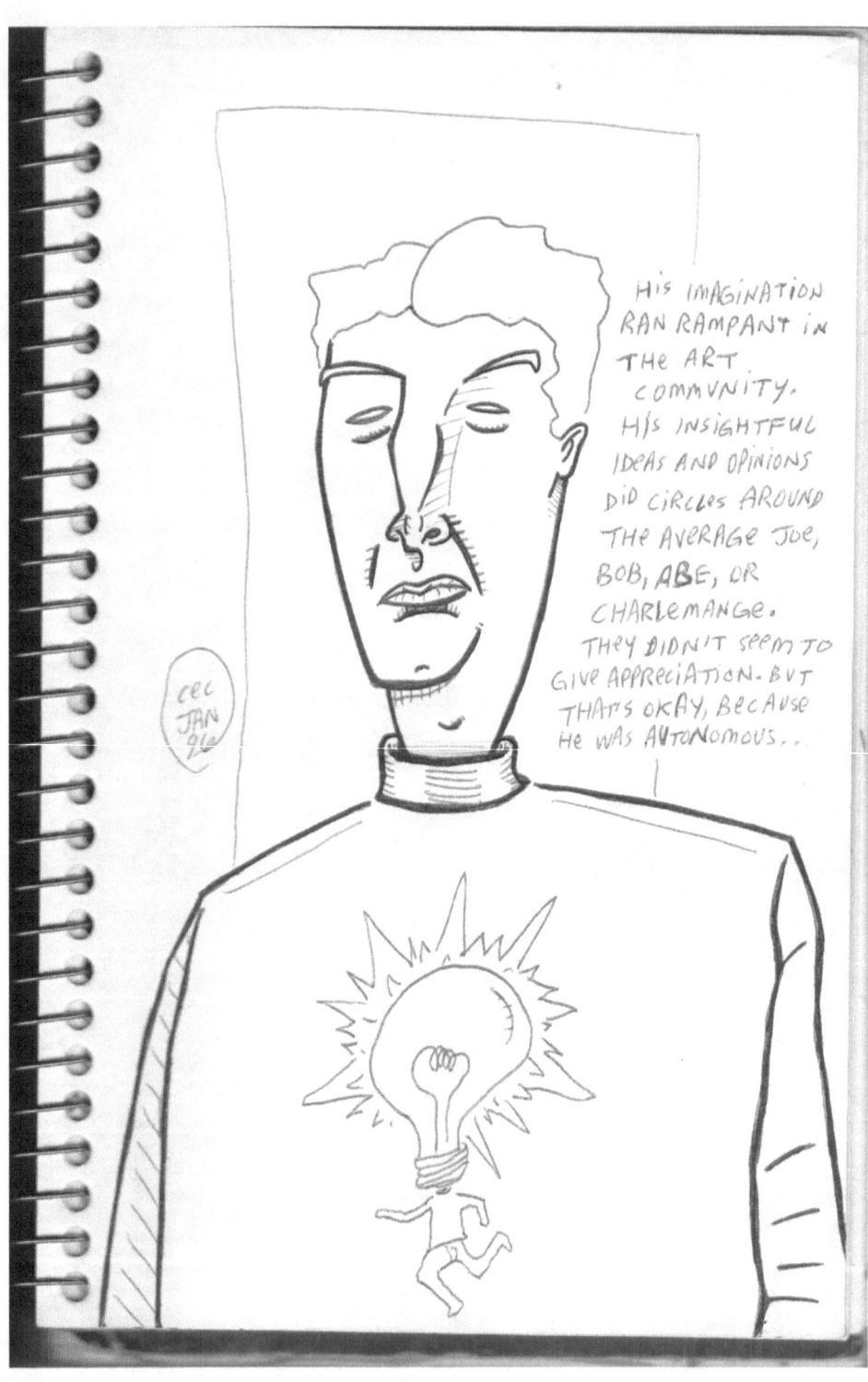

even

pictures

taking

and

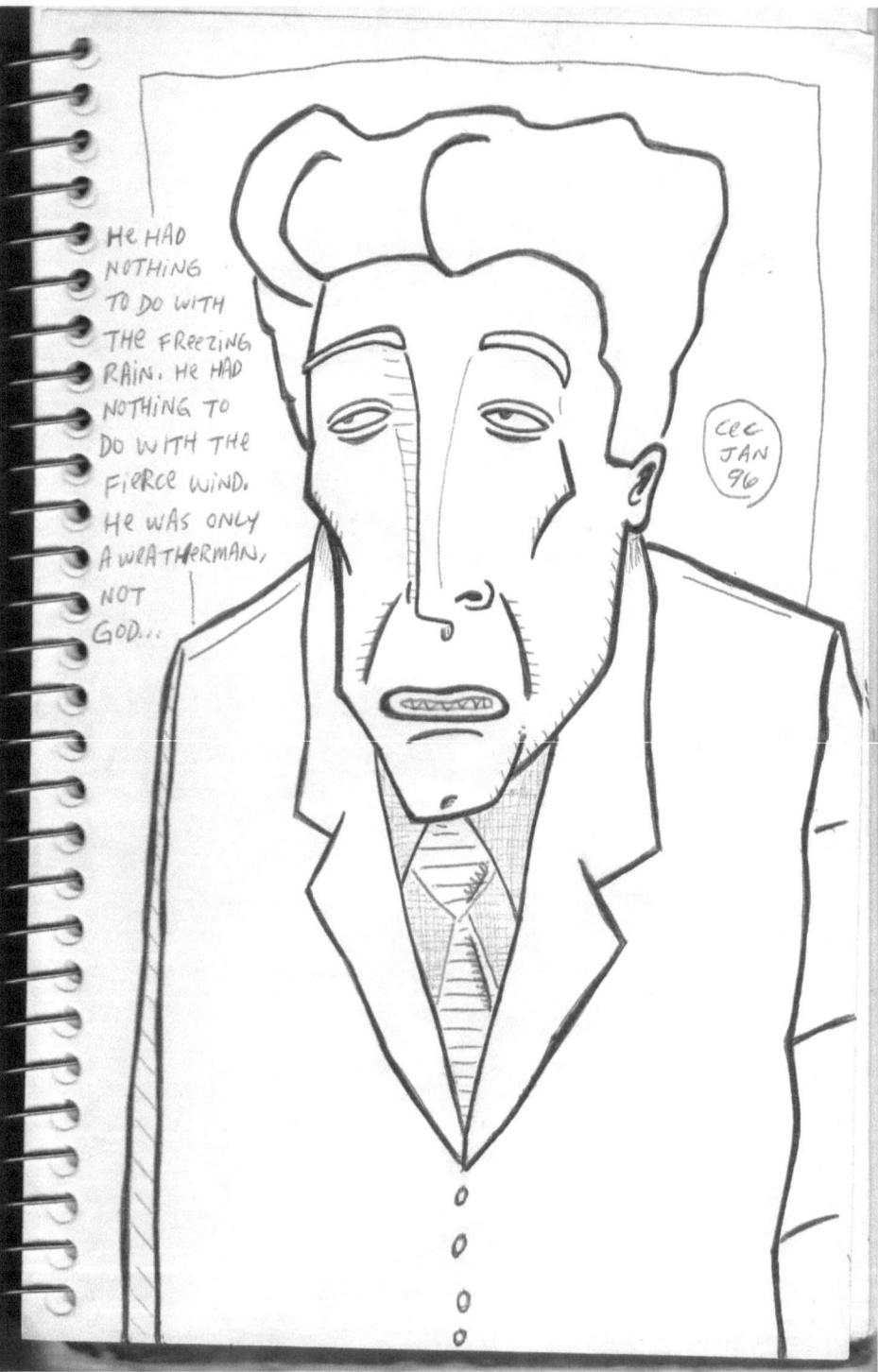

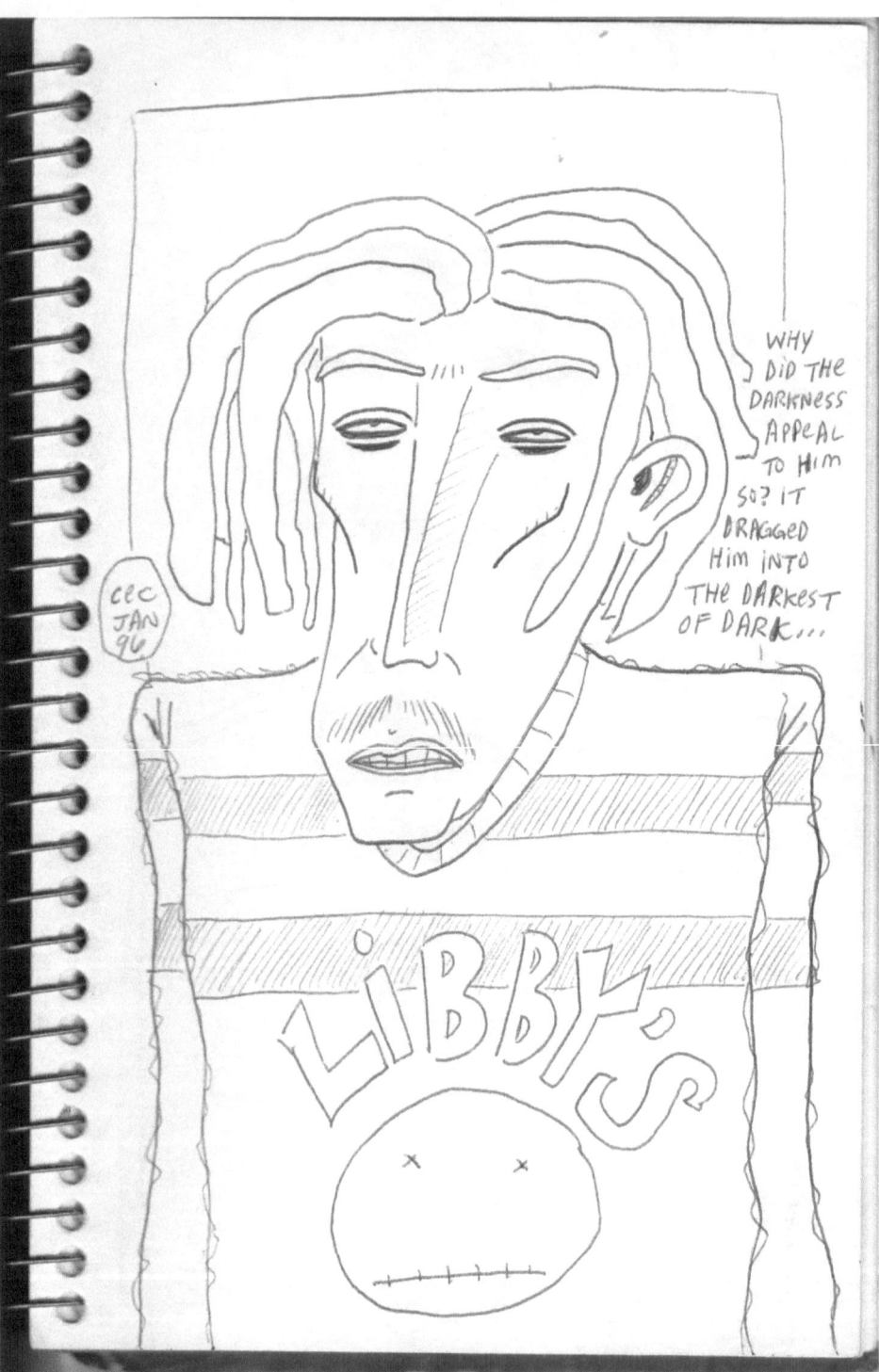

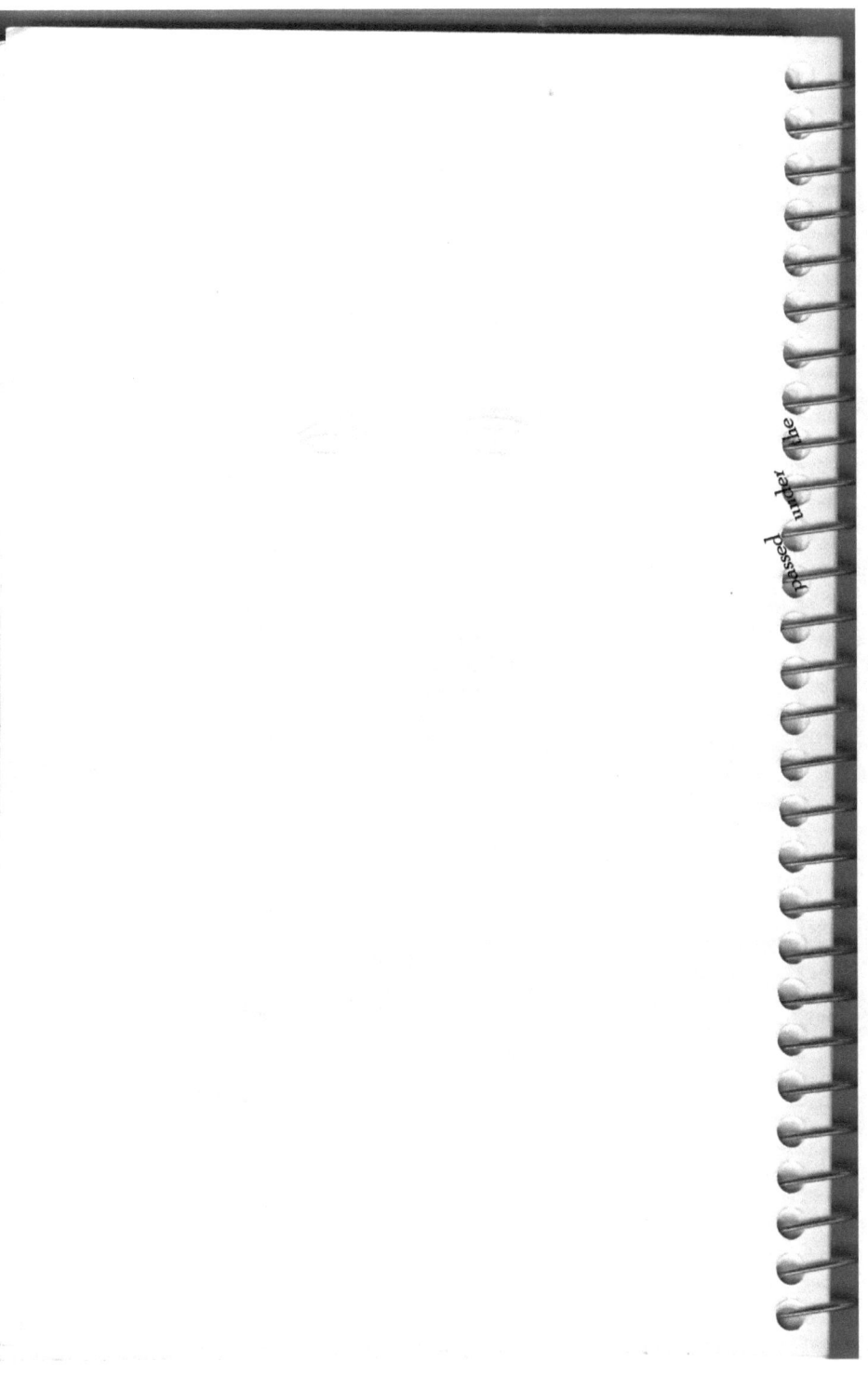

passed under the under passed

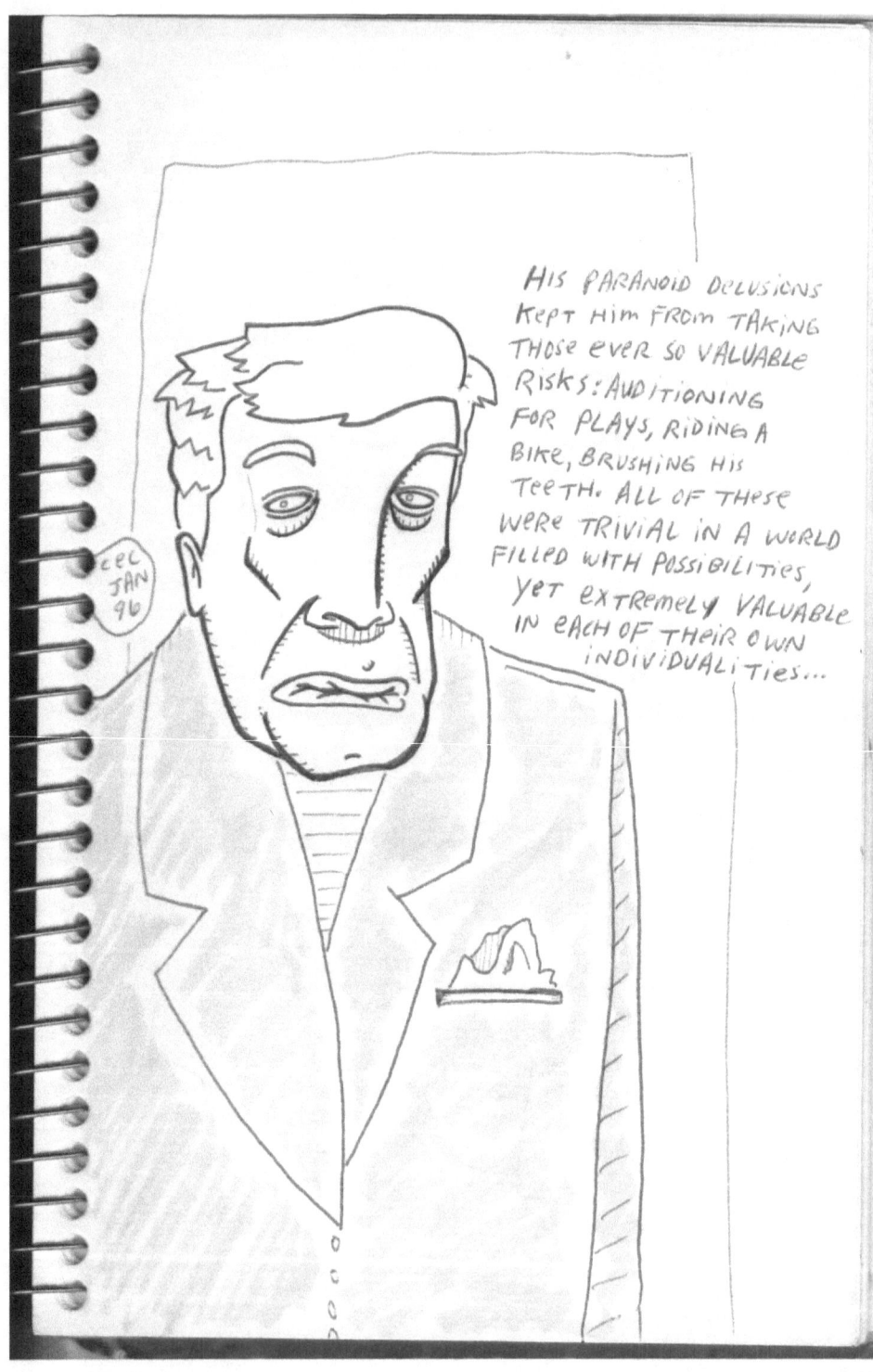

bridge and is now

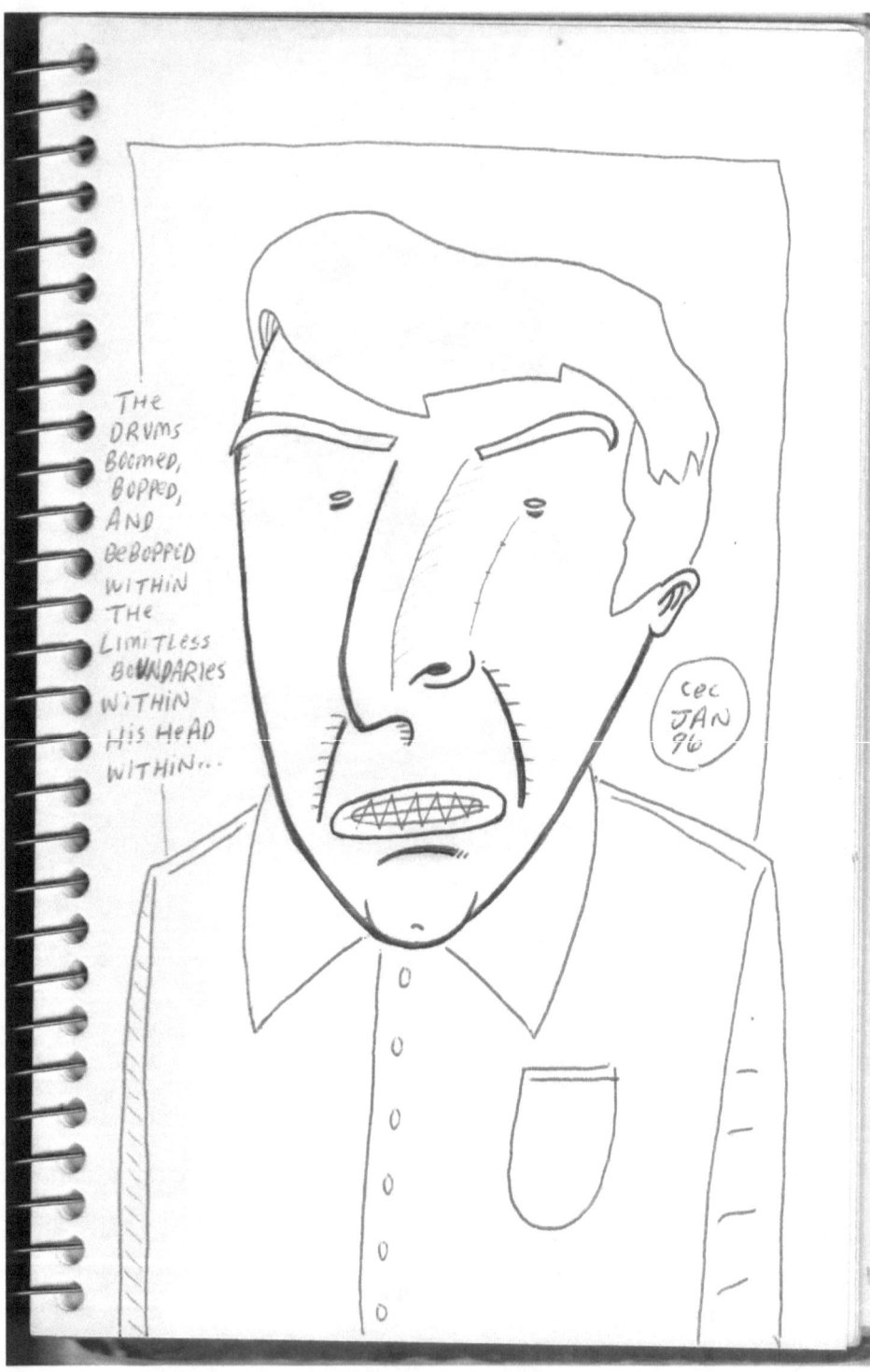

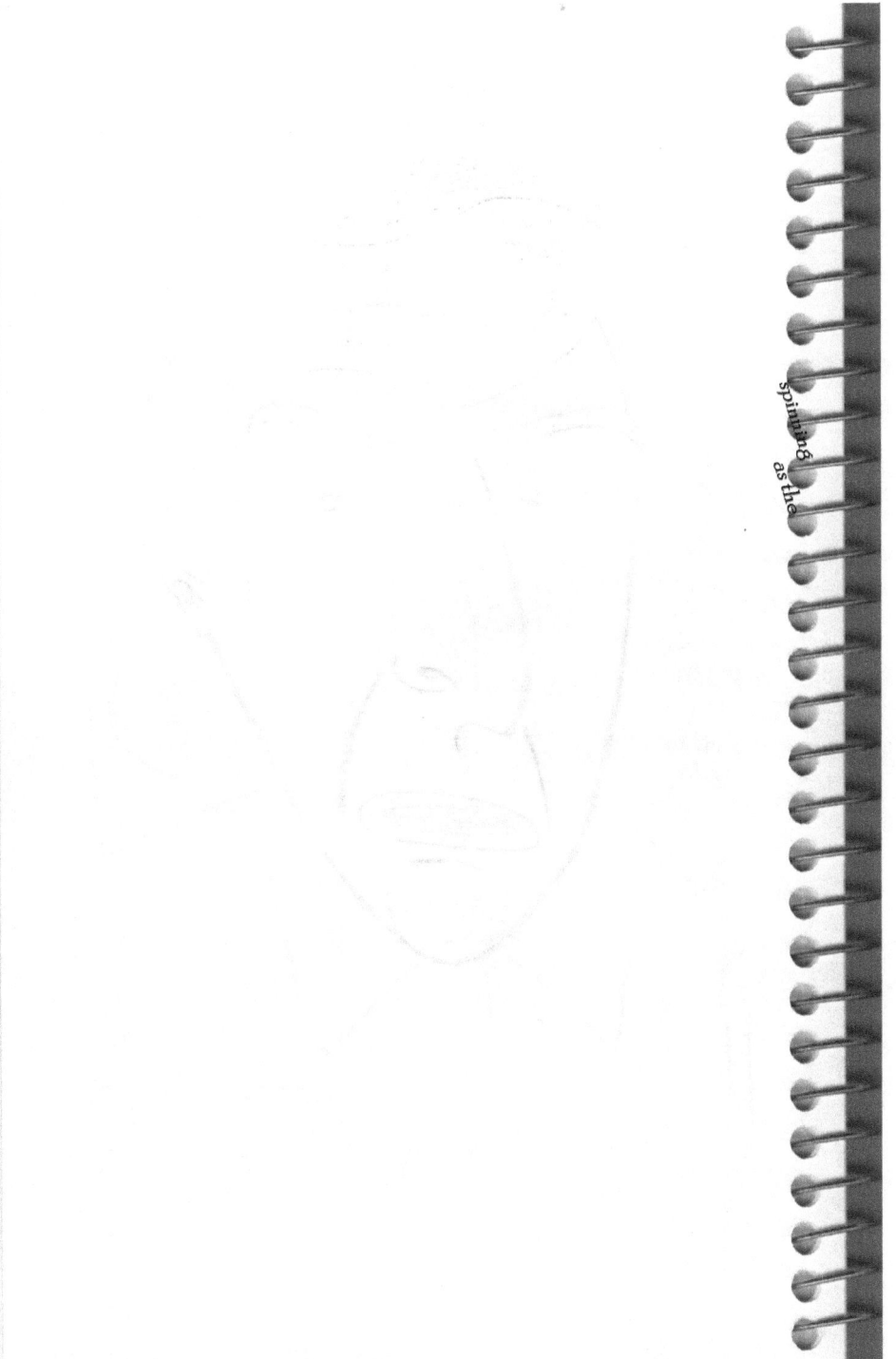

spinning
as the

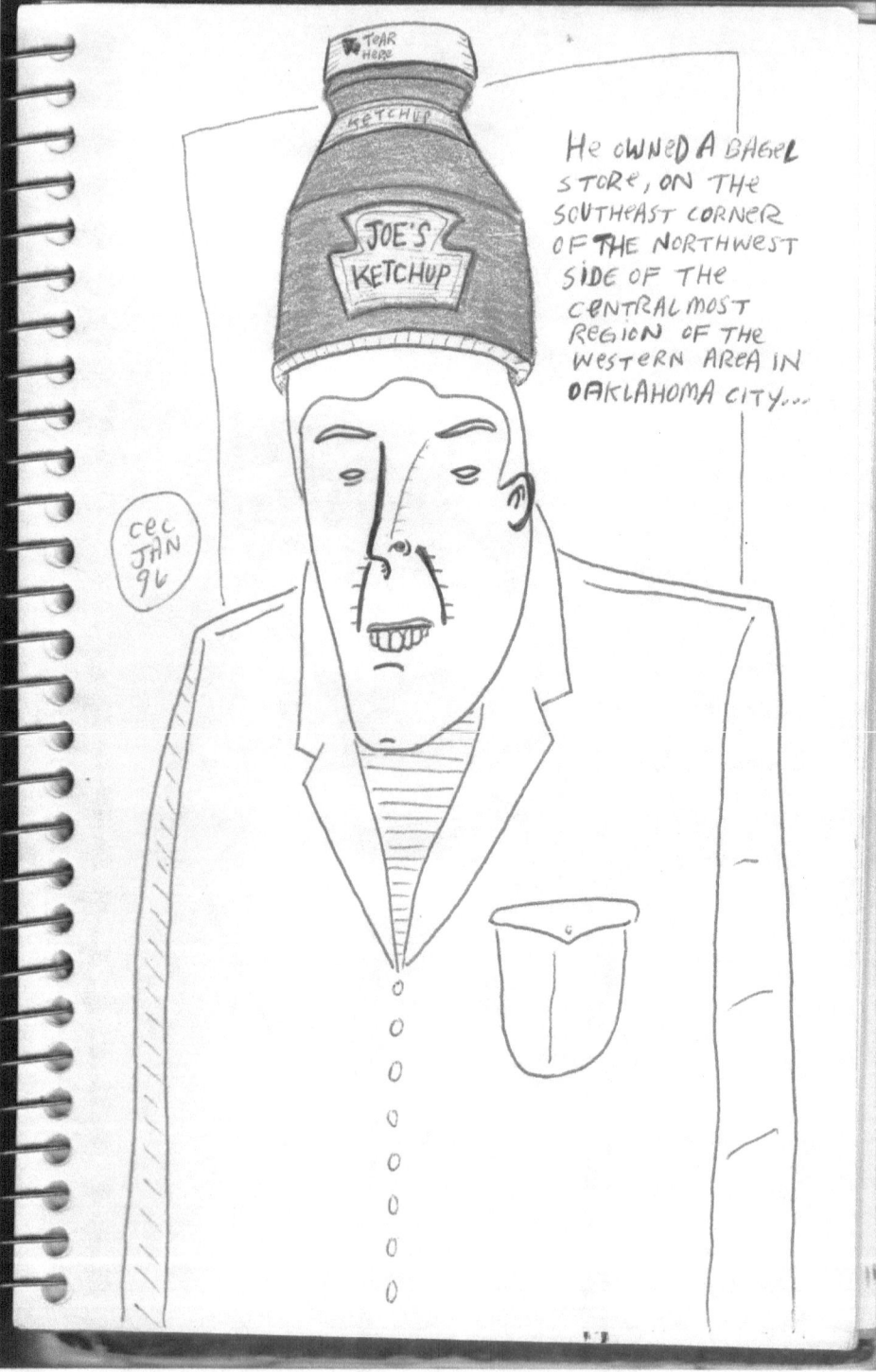

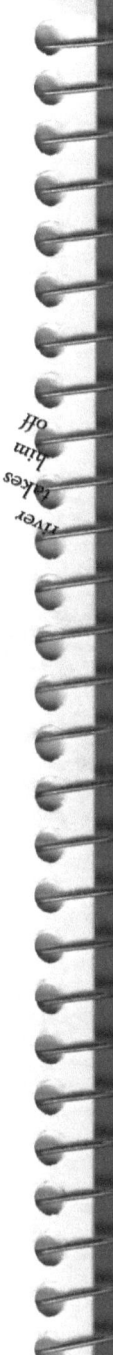

river takes him off

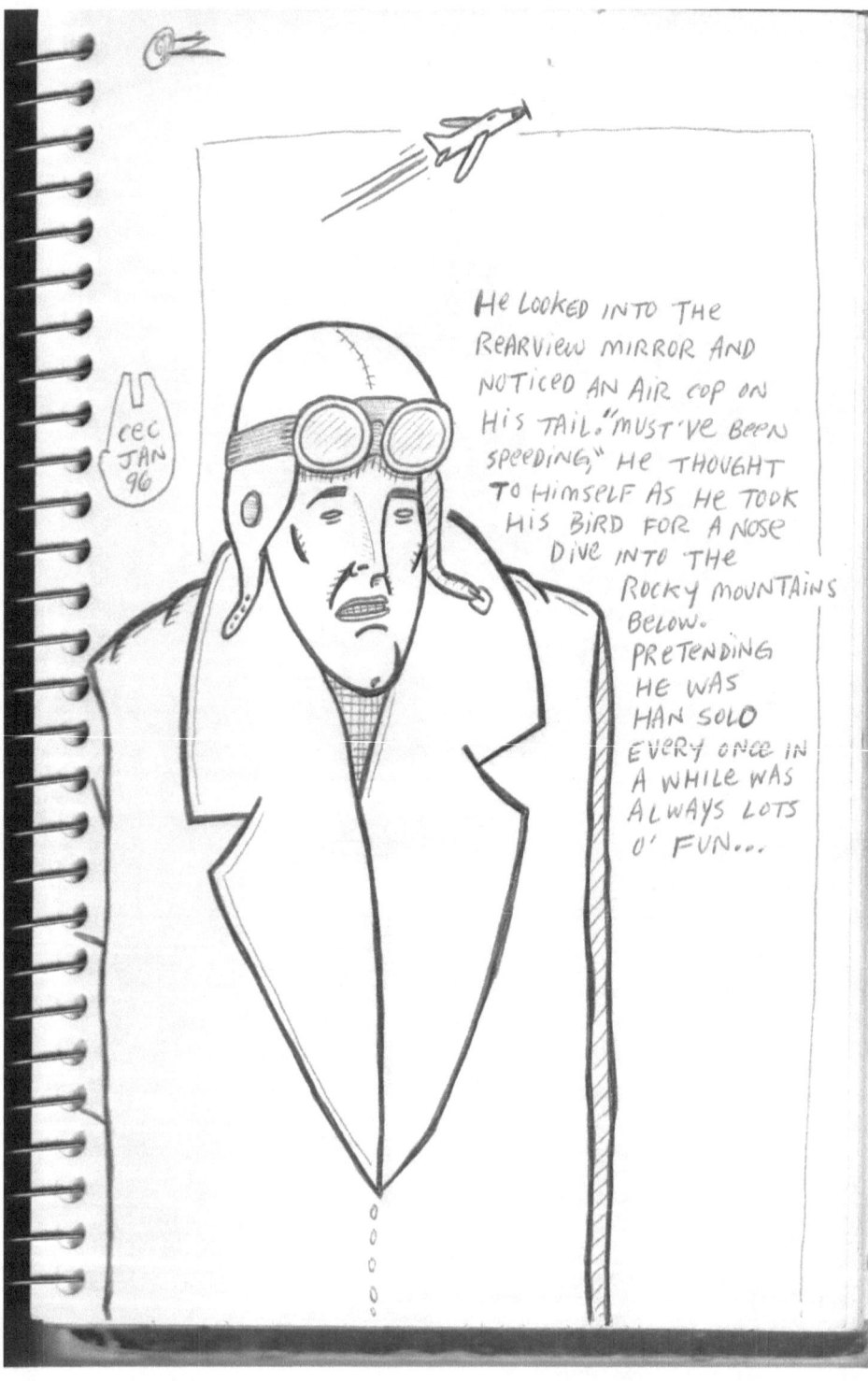

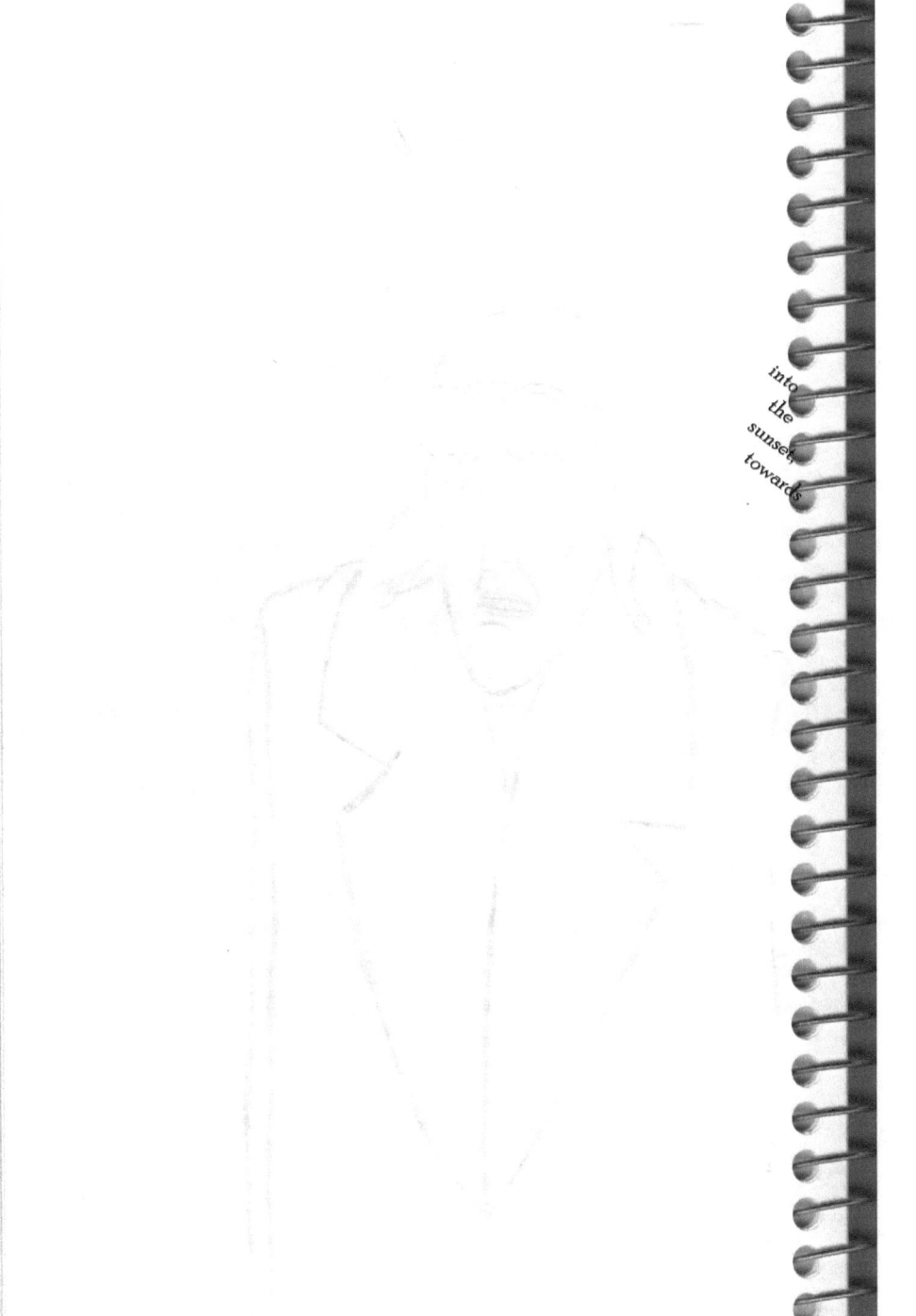

into
the
sunset,
towards

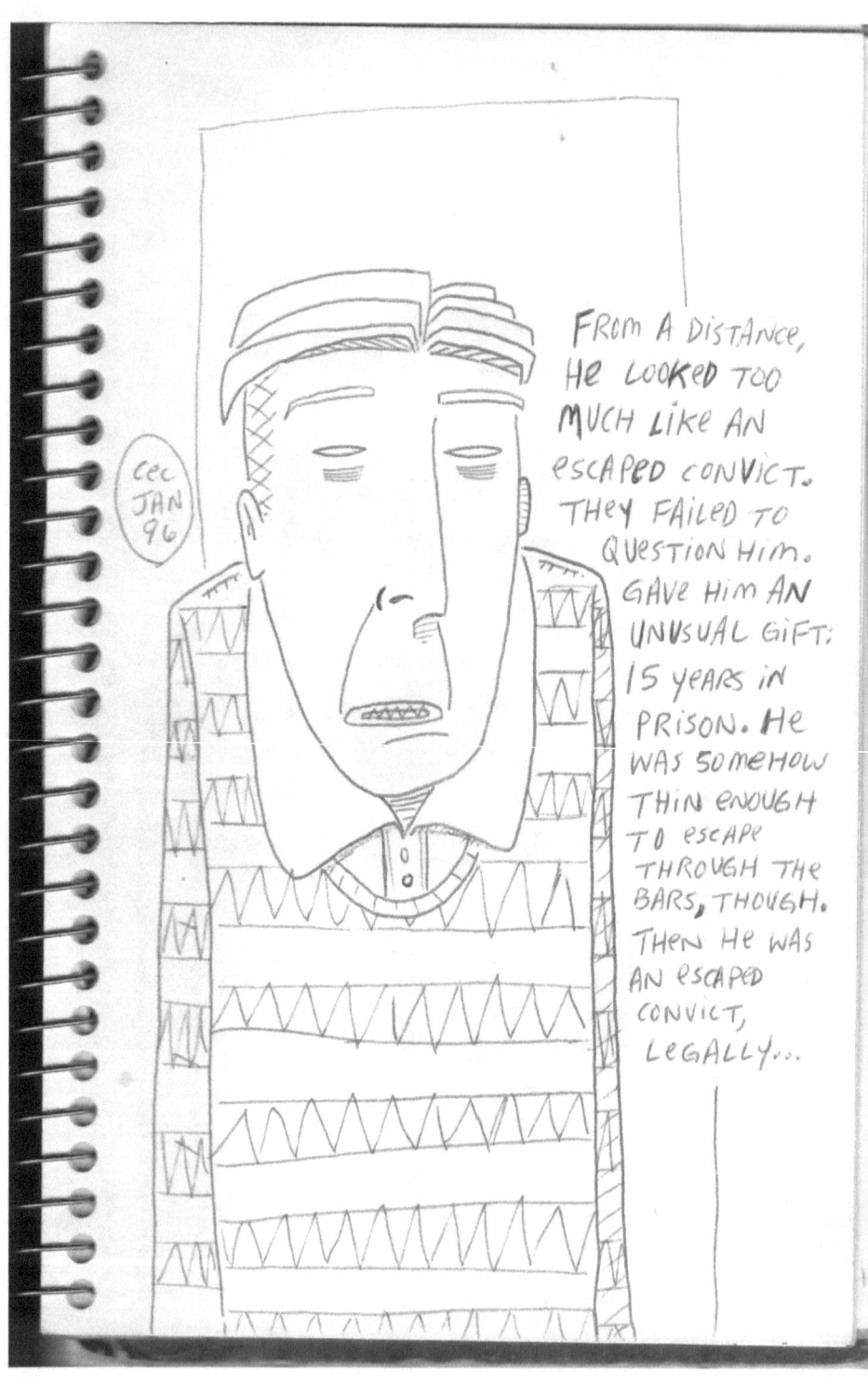

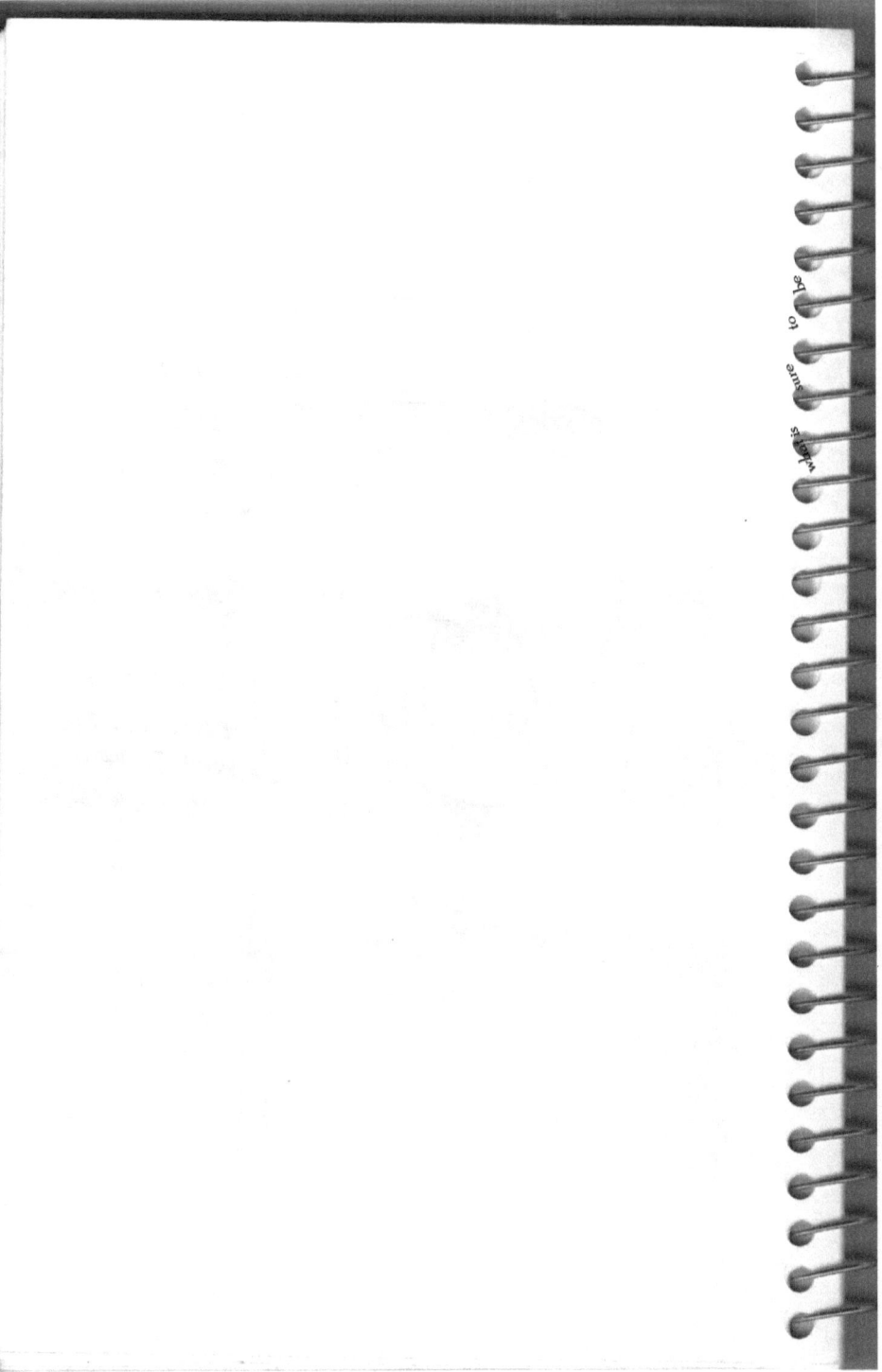

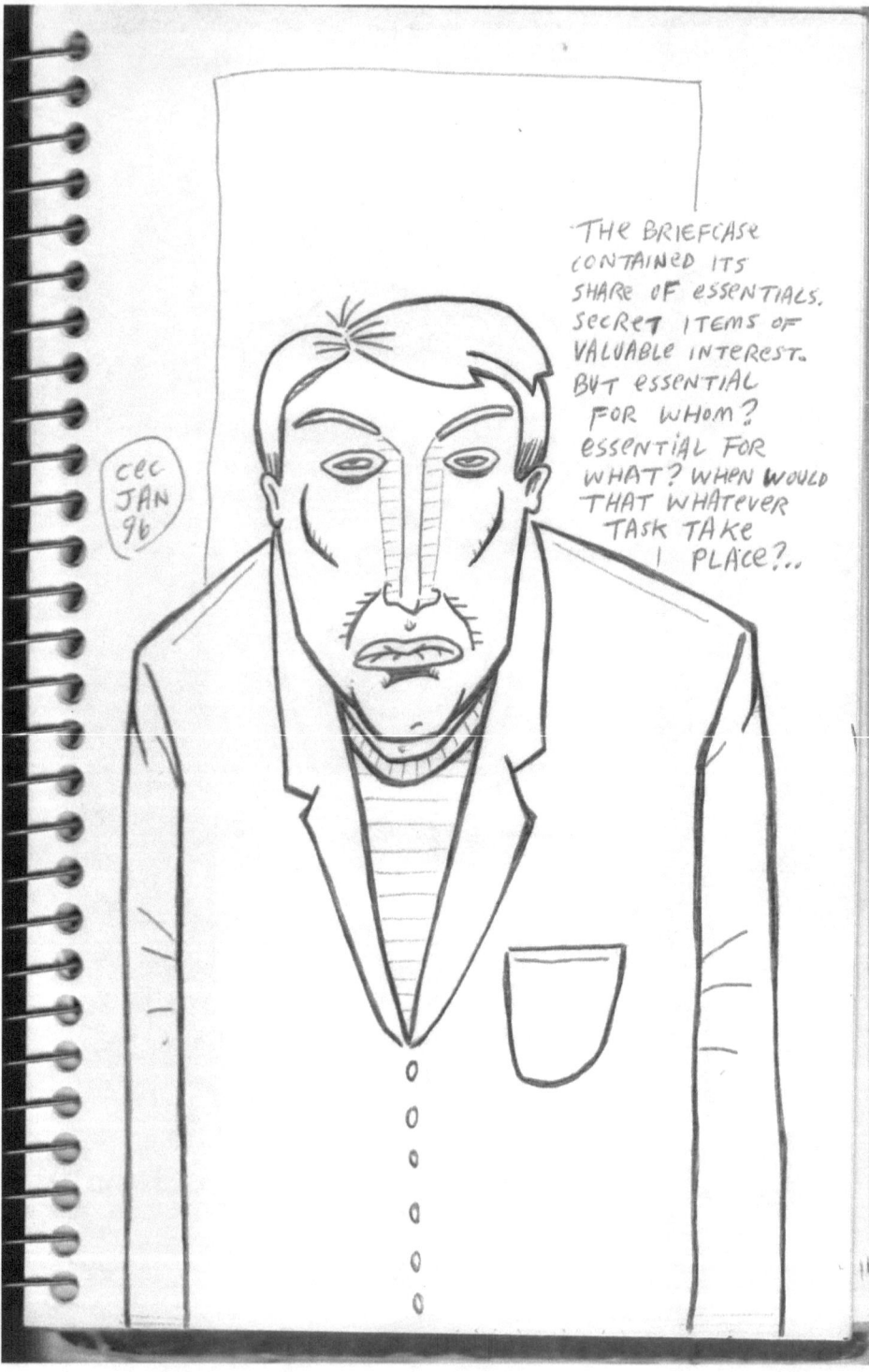

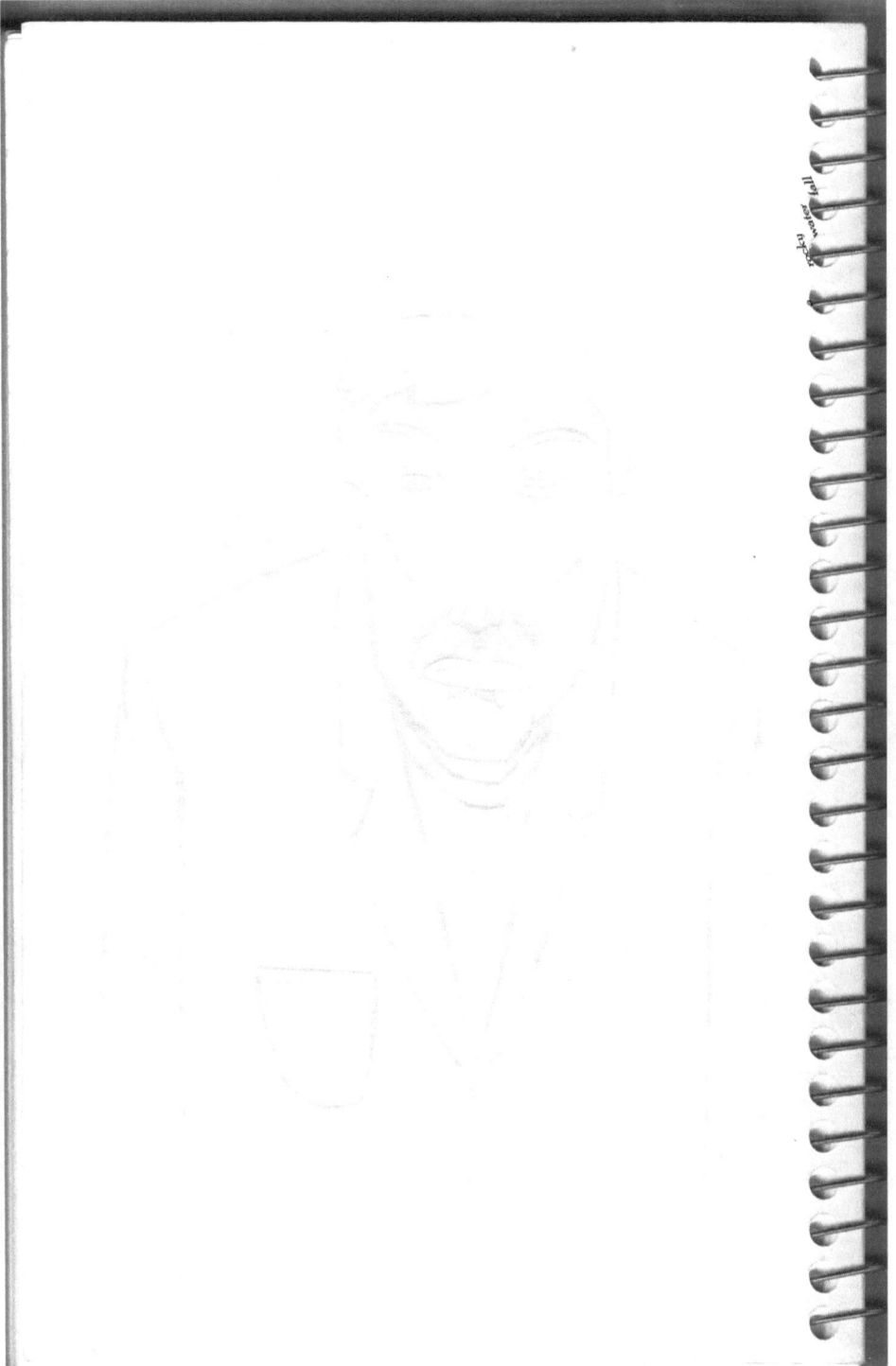

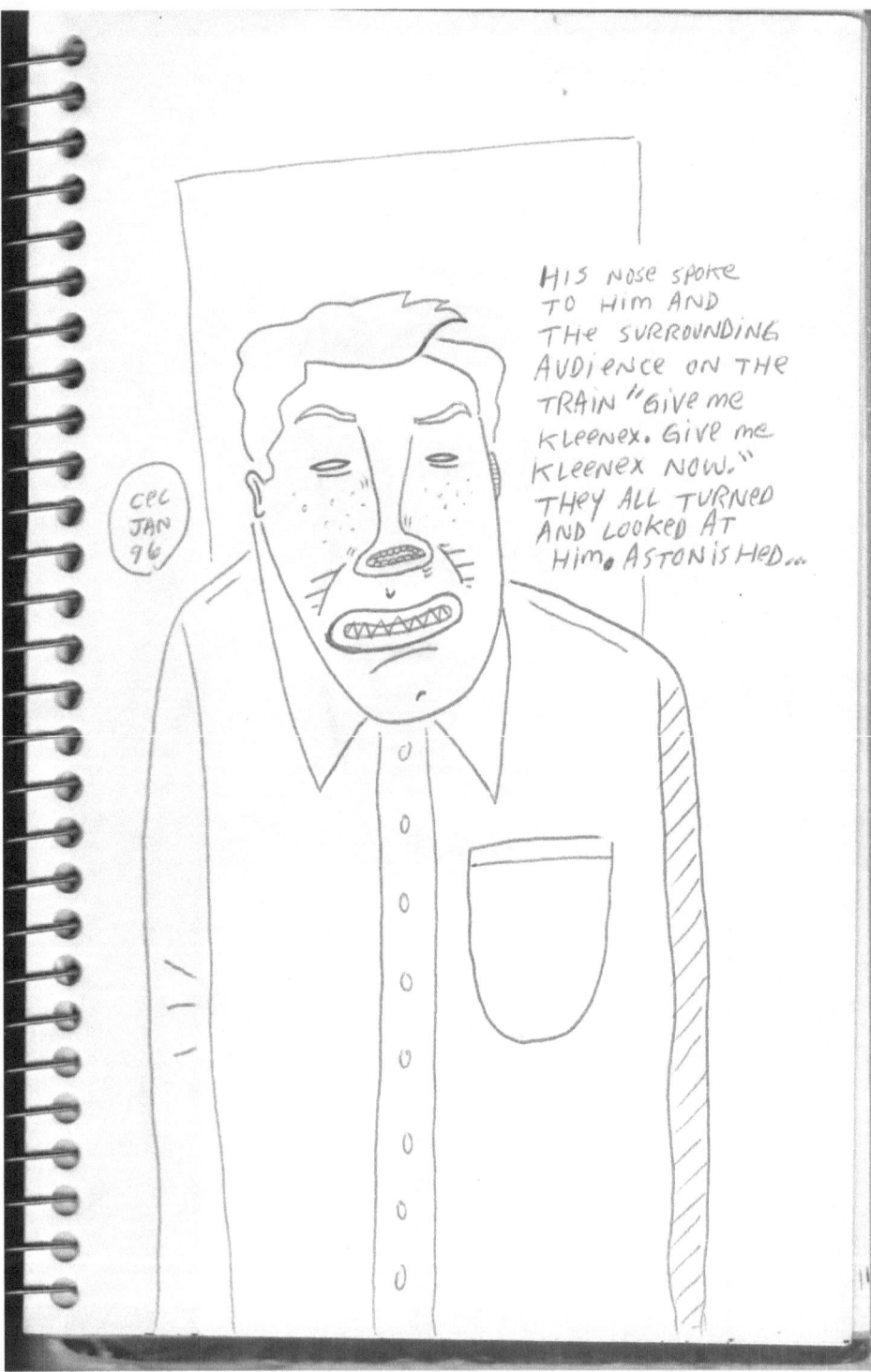

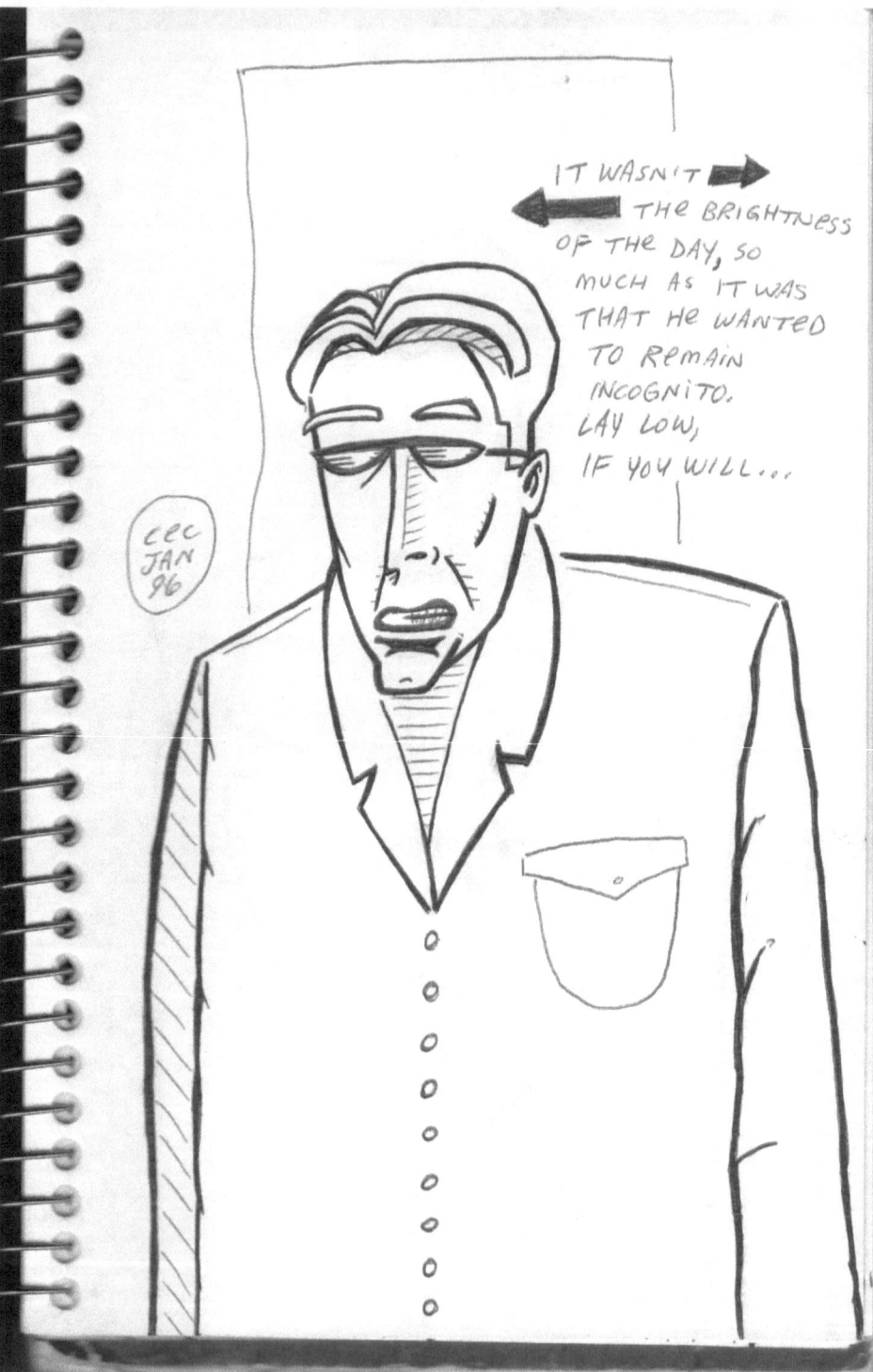

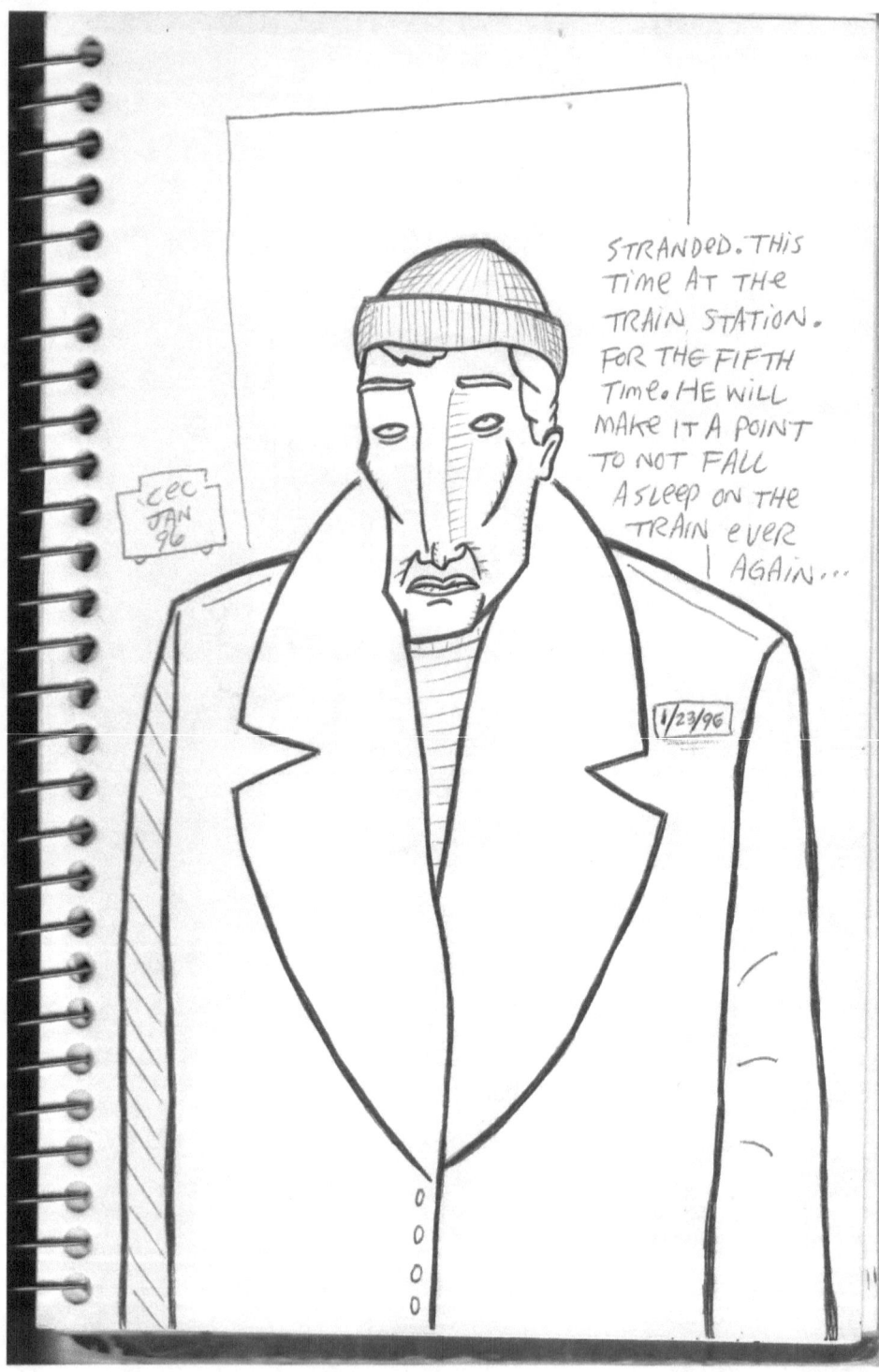

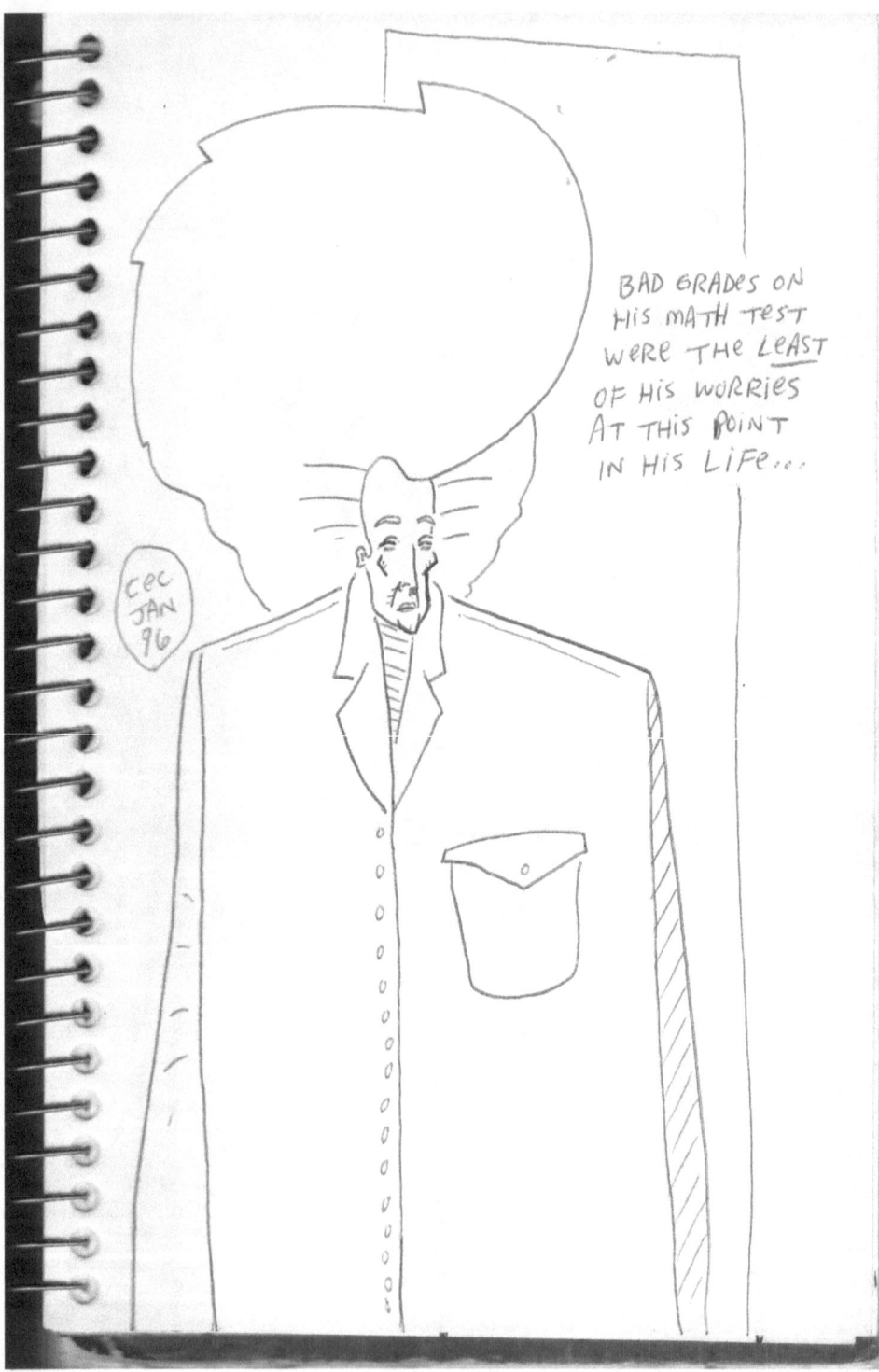

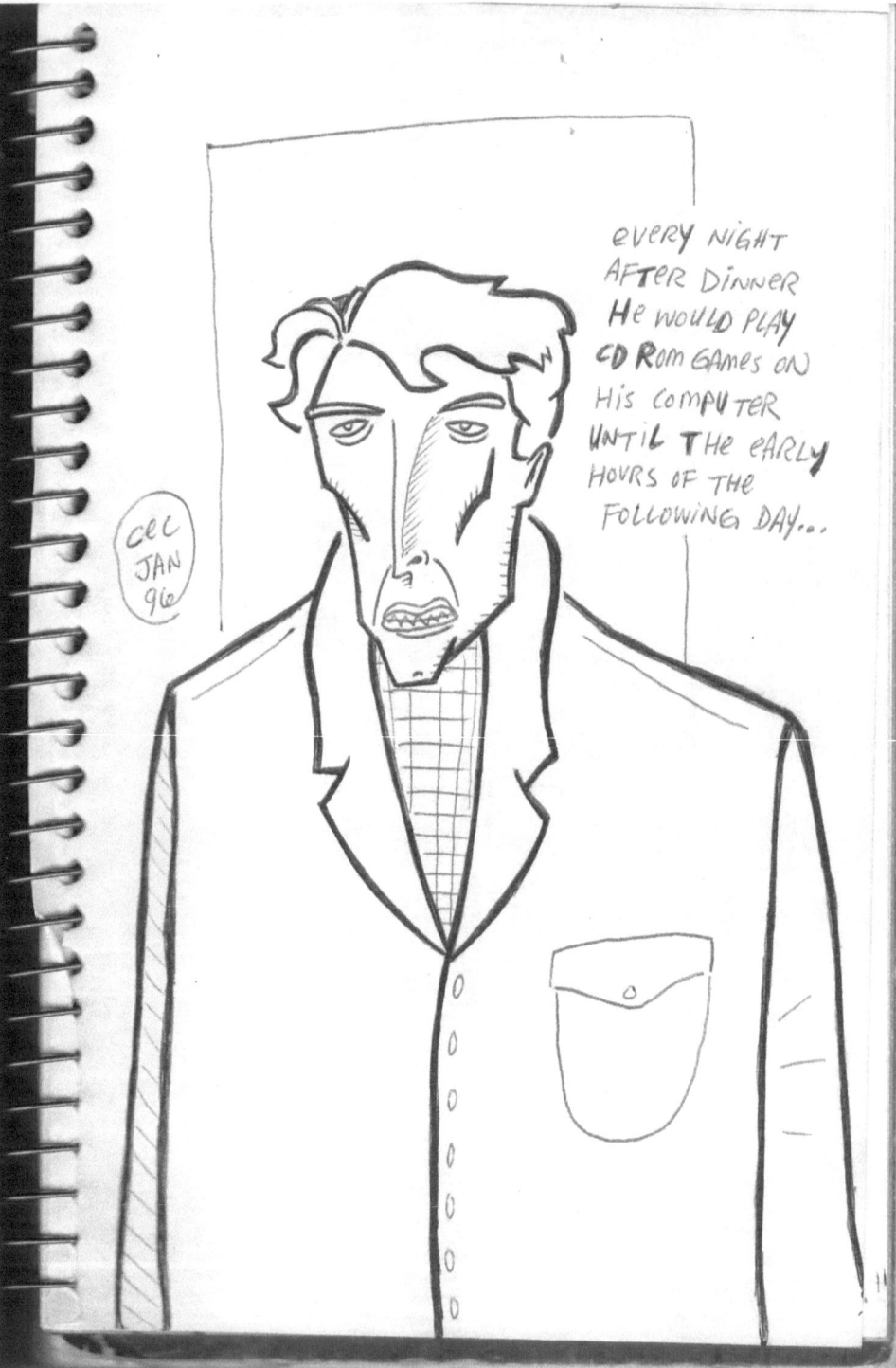

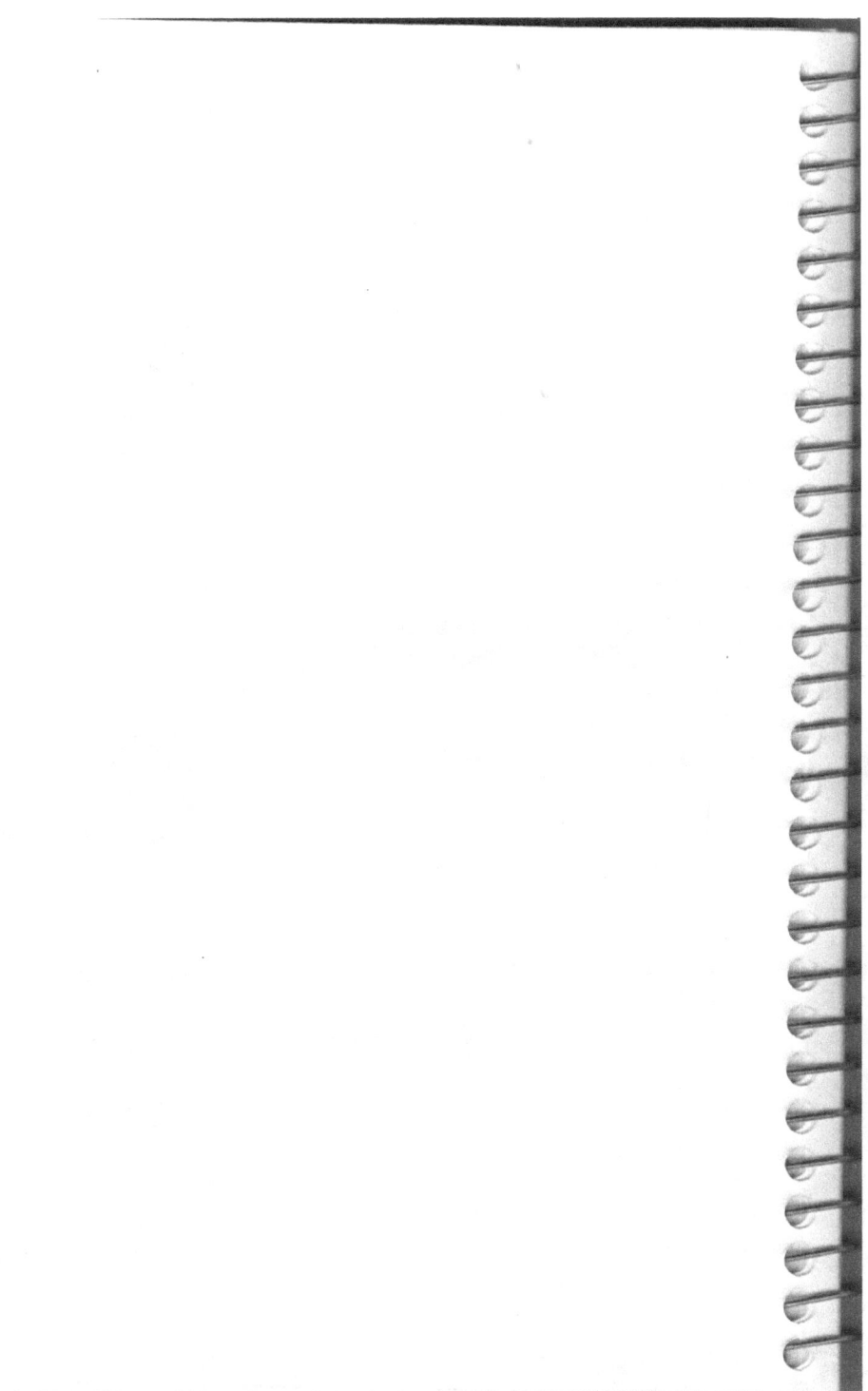

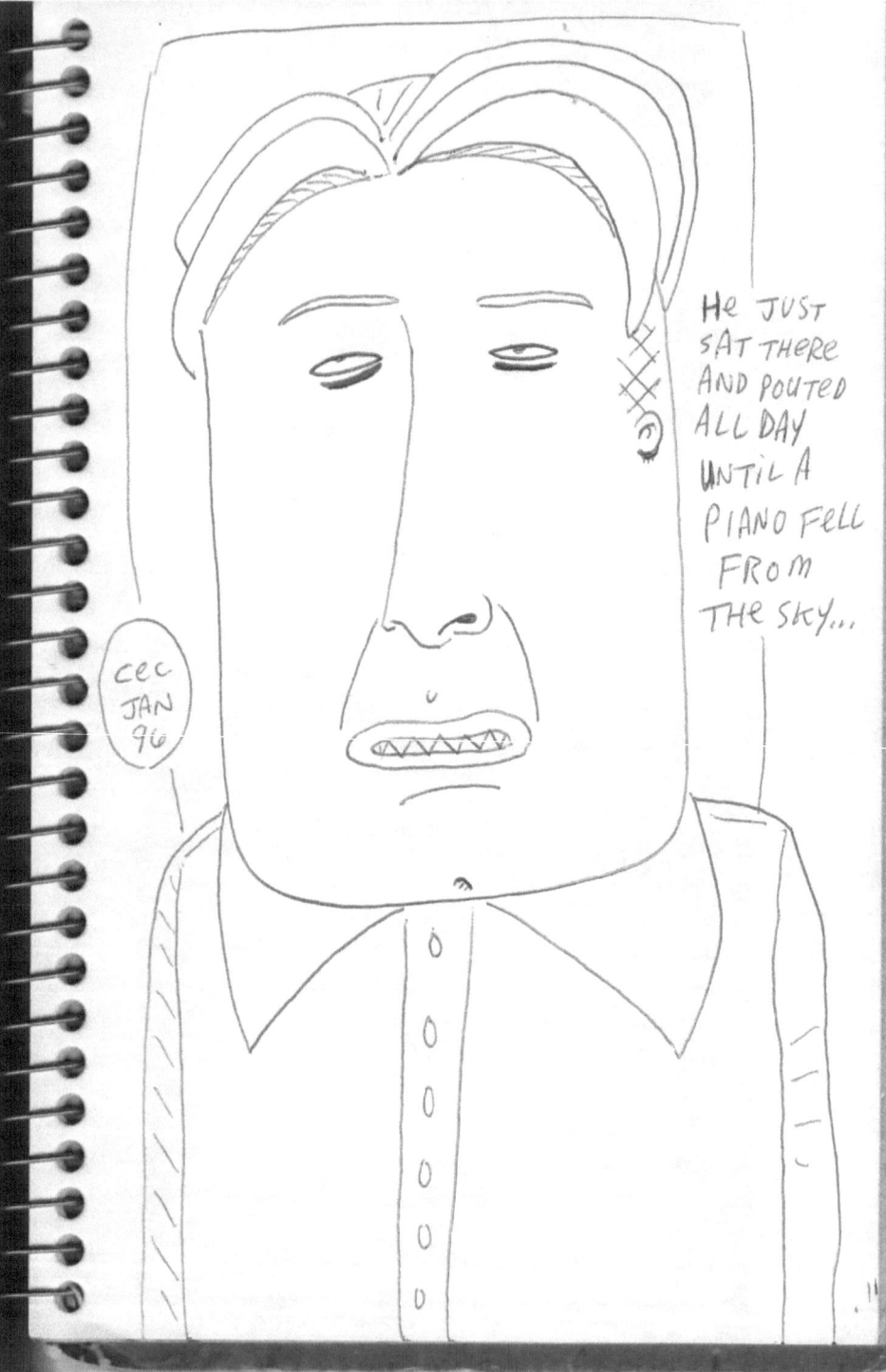

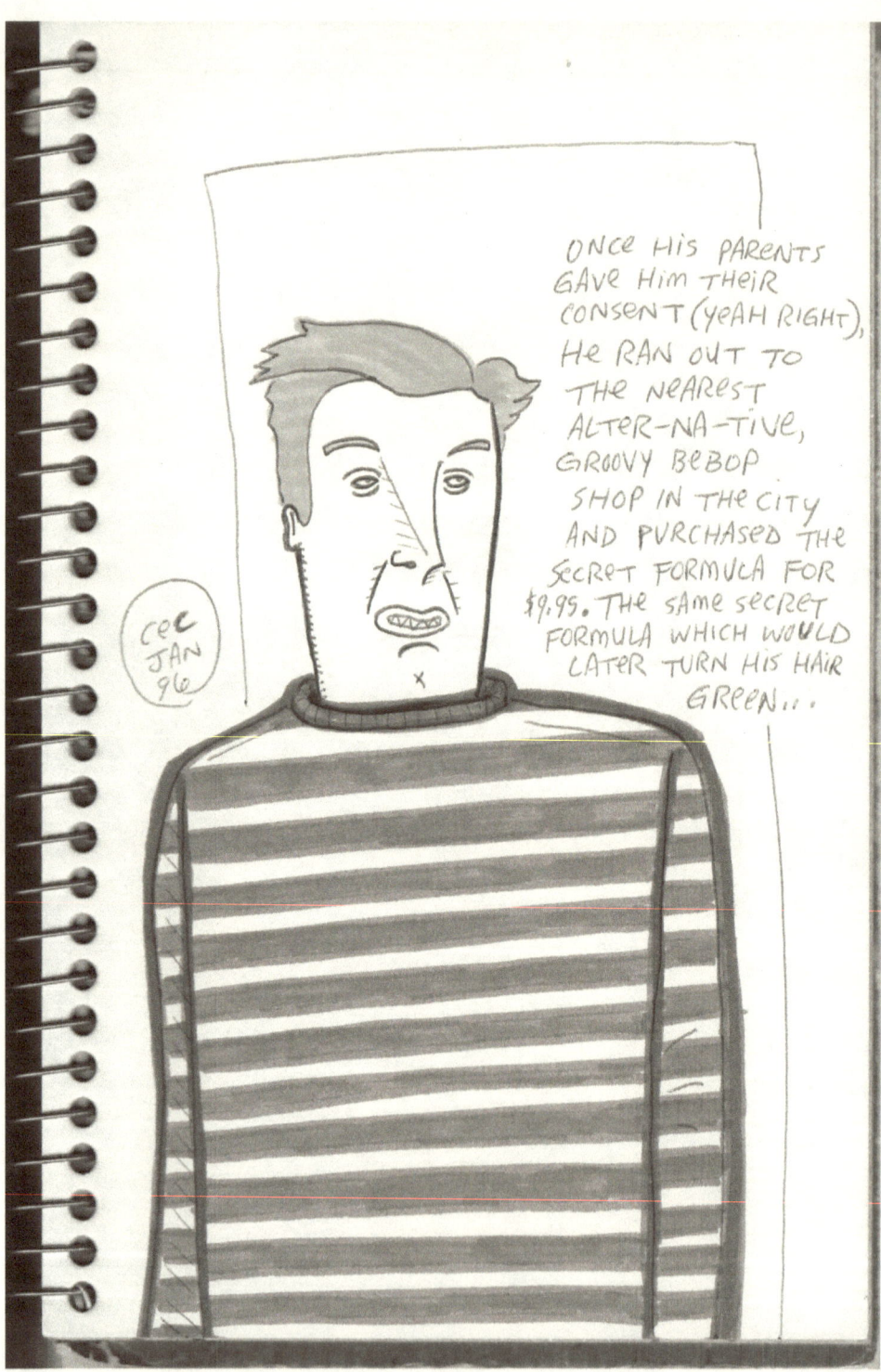

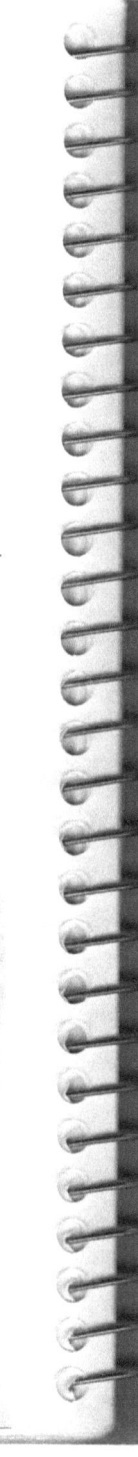

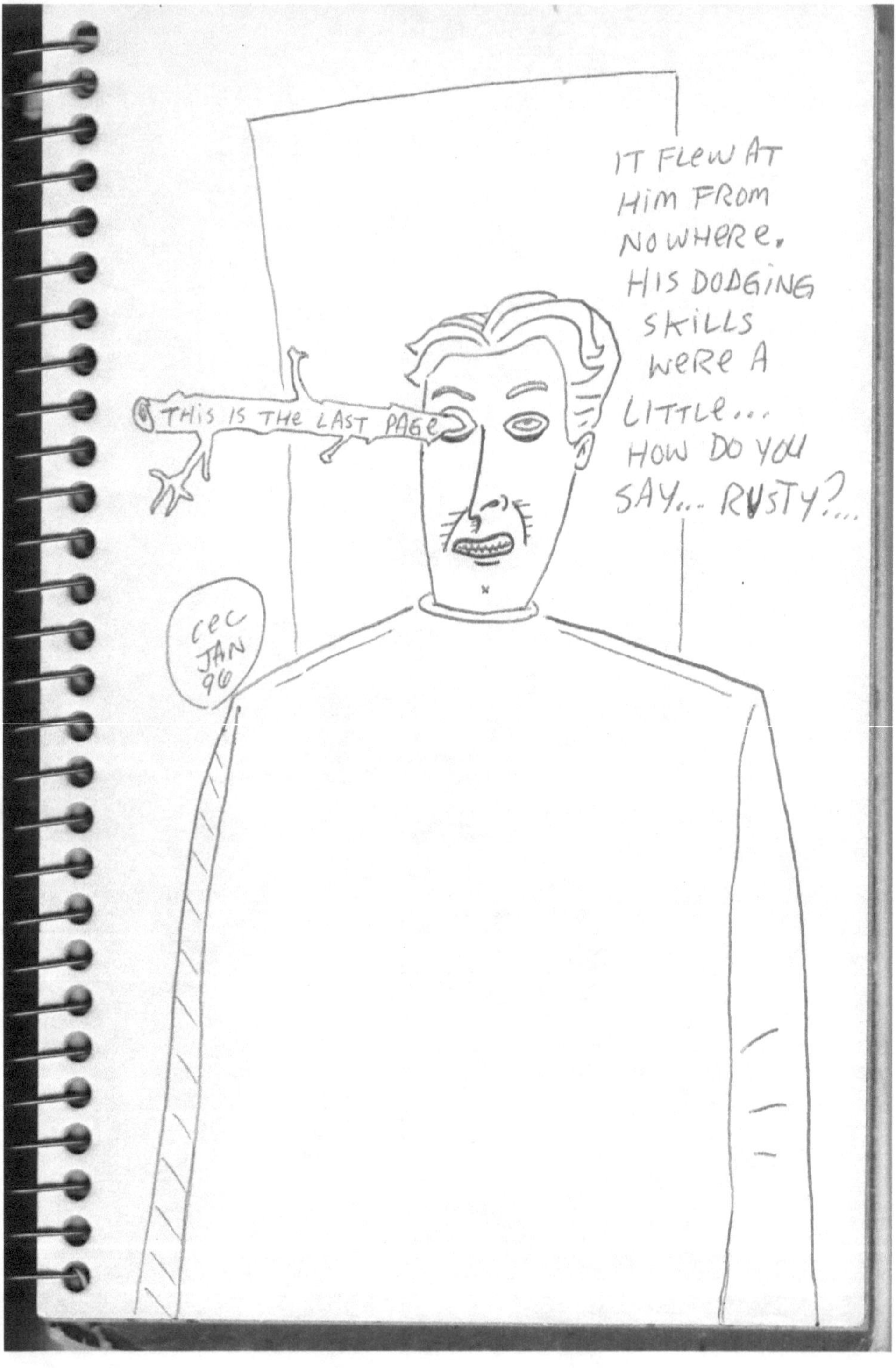
IT FLEW AT HIM FROM NOWHERE. HIS DODGING SKILLS WERE A LITTLE... HOW DO YOU SAY... RUSTY?...
THIS IS THE LAST PAGE
CEC JAN 96

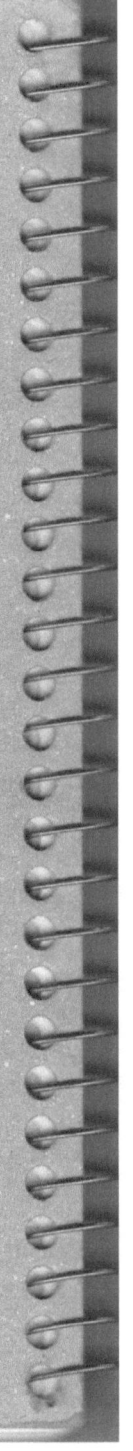

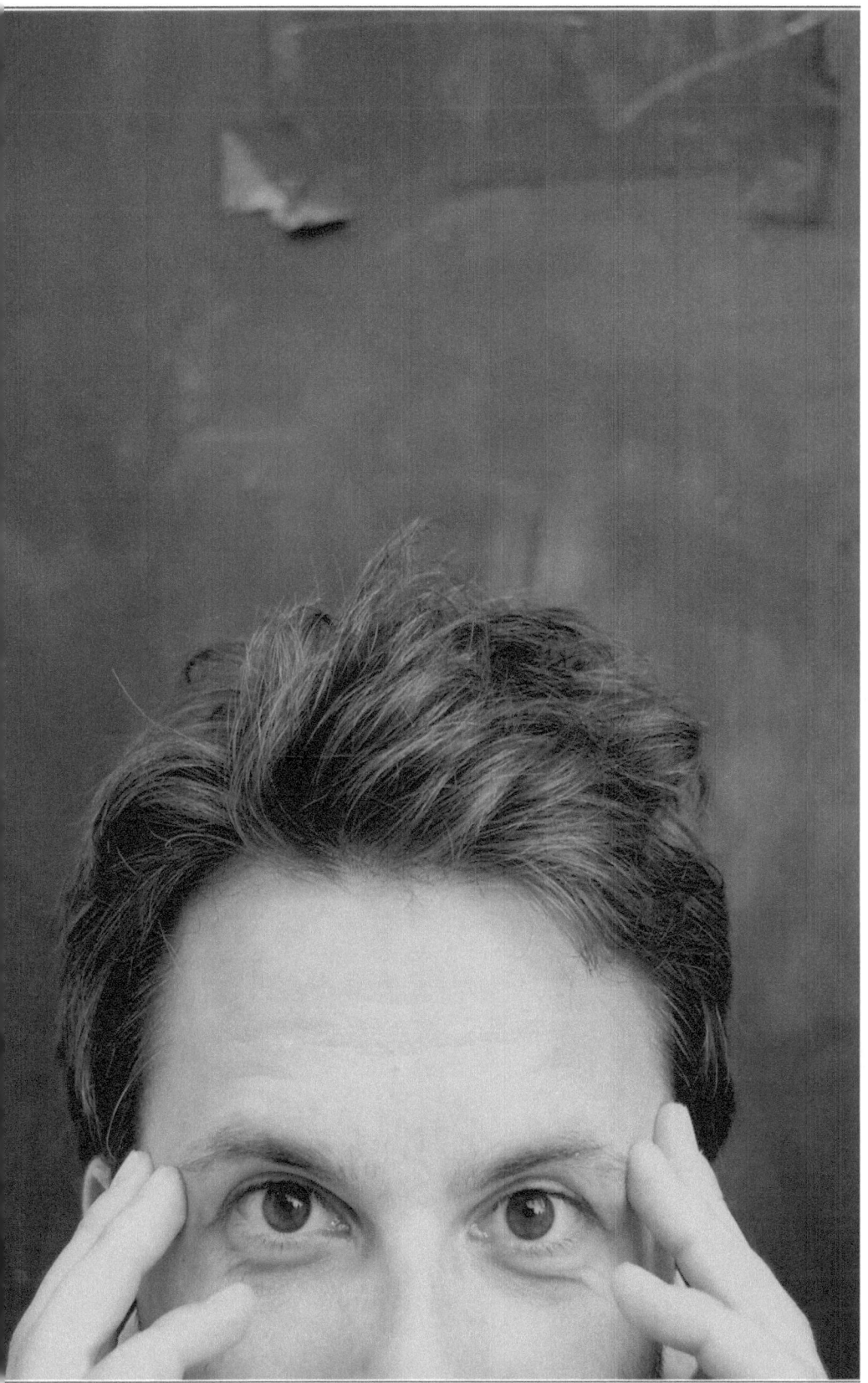

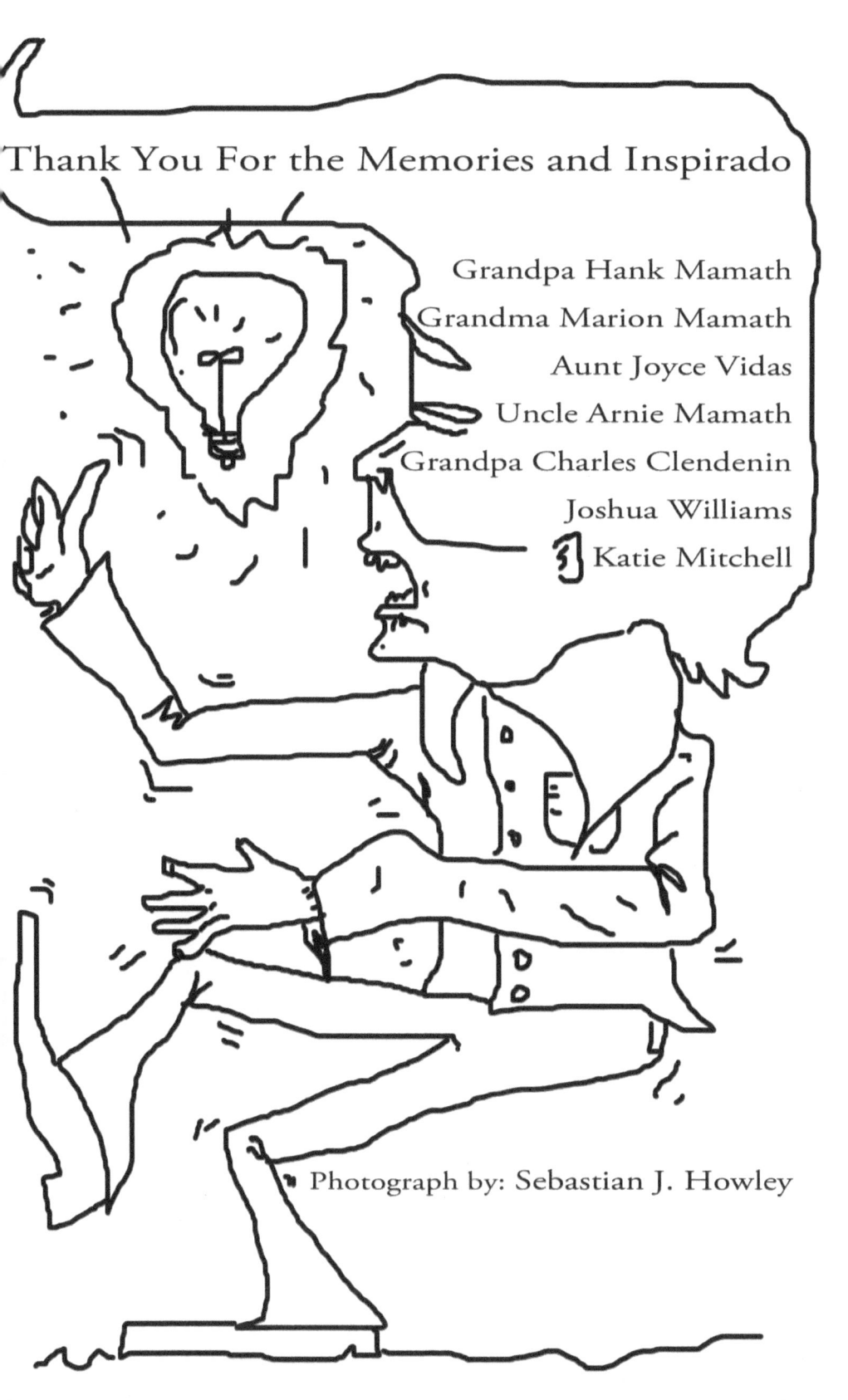

Thank You For the Memories and Inspirado

Grandpa Hank Mamath
Grandma Marion Mamath
Aunt Joyce Vidas
Uncle Arnie Mamath
Grandpa Charles Clendenin
Joshua Williams
Katie Mitchell

Photograph by: Sebastian J. Howley

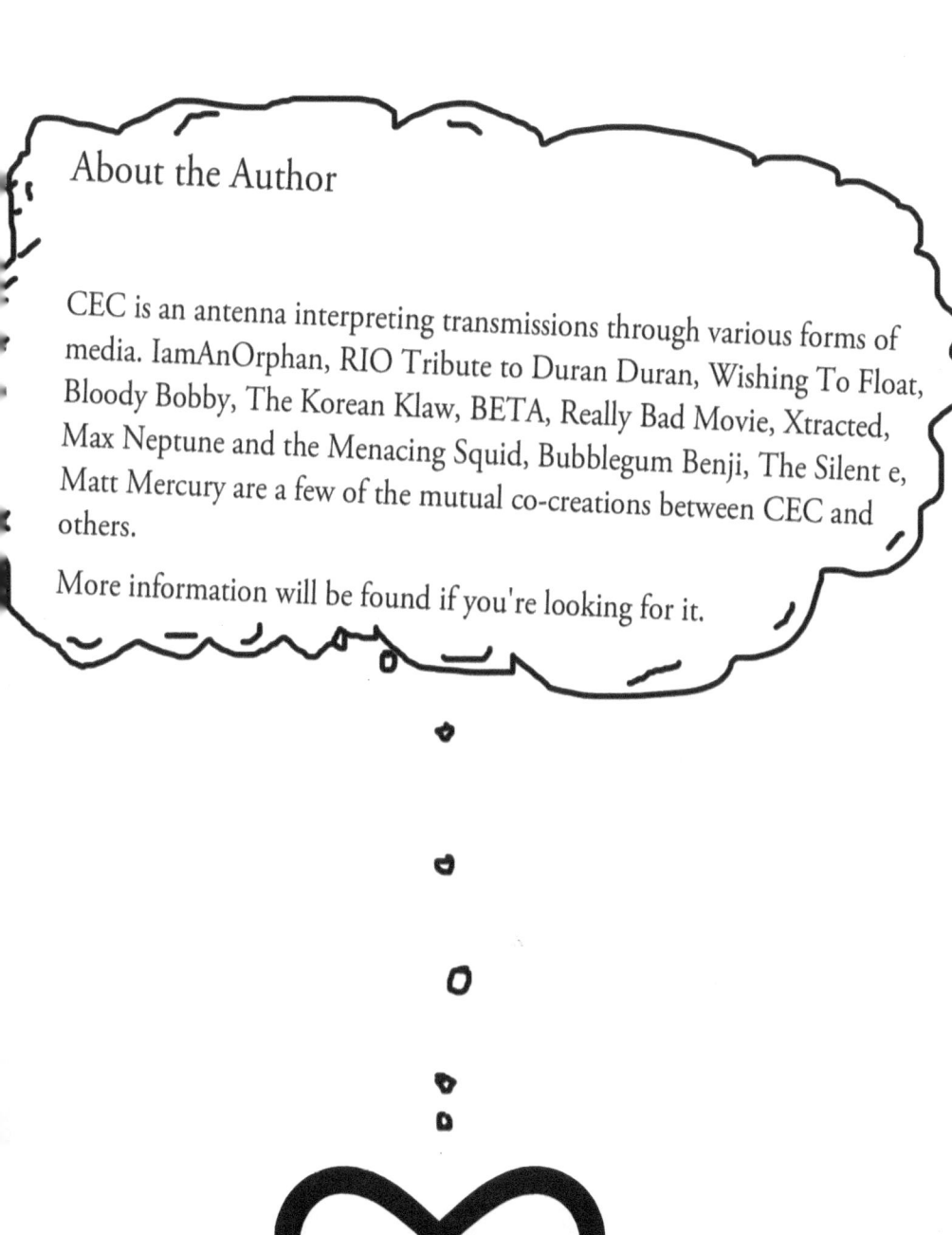

About the Author

CEC is an antenna interpreting transmissions through various forms of media. IamAnOrphan, RIO Tribute to Duran Duran, Wishing To Float, Bloody Bobby, The Korean Klaw, BETA, Really Bad Movie, Xtracted, Max Neptune and the Menacing Squid, Bubblegum Benji, The Silent e, Matt Mercury are a few of the mutual co-creations between CEC and others.

More information will be found if you're looking for it.

Do you have ideas for stories involving these characters? Email a jpeg of the character and your story to: cecthemoment@gmail.com for a chance to be included in a new book.

www.ingramcontent.com/pod-product-compliance
Lightning Source LLC
Chambersburg PA
CBHW032024170526
45157CB00002B/842